BRAIN STATES

Tom Kenyon, M.A.

Published by: United States Publishing
3485 Mercantile Avenue
Naples, Florida 33942

Cover Art: "Knower, Sage of Crystals," from the Voyager
Tarot by James Wanless & Ken Knutson
© Merrill-West Publishing, 1984

Illustrations by: Patty Smith

Printed in the United States of America

Library of Congress Cataloging-in-Publication Data

Kenyon, Tom.
   Brain States / Tom Kenyon.
      p.   cm.
   ISBN 1-880698-04-8 : $11.95
   1. Self-actualization (Psychology) 2. Altered states of consciousness. I. Title.
BF637.S4K46 1994
154.4 — dc20   93-23667
                   CIP

I dedicate this book to Pam,
best friend, confidant, lover, wife.

About the Author

Tom Kenyon, M.A., is the founder and director of Acoustic Brain Research Inc., a recognized leader in psychoacoustic research and development. Mr. Kenyon created ABR in 1983 to scientifically document the effects of sound, music, and language on the human nervous system and on human behavior. Mr. Kenyon holds a master's degree in psychological counseling from Columbia Pacific University and has more than ten years of clinical experience as a psychotherapist. He is also certified in Whole Brain Learning and NeuroLinguistic Programming and has extensive training in Ericksonian hypnosis. Through the use of hypnotic states and sound healing, Mr. Kenyon has created methods that accelerate therapy and behavioral changes. In 1987, he synthesized this portion of his work into a therapeutic modality called Body/Mind Re-education.® He currently conducts professional certification programs for therapists and counselors in this form of rapid psychotherapy and in a new form of brain development training called Interdimensional Consciousness Training, which stimulates unused portions of the brain/mind. Mr. Kenyon is available for speaking engagements and seminars. Please contact him through Acoustic Brain Research Inc., P.O. Box 168, Deer Harbor WA 98243.

Contents

Foreword

F or the last year and a half, I have worked on this manuscript at a feverish pace. I would write on weekends, late at night, and sometimes sandwiched between clients. I wrote parts at 30,000 feet on cross-country plane flights.

My efforts were driven by a recognition that wherever I taught there was a general misunderstanding about altered states of awareness, and that some of these errors were actually hindering people in their personal growth and, in some cases, posing serious dangers.

This book is a humble attempt to correct some of this misinformation and to give readers practical tools that they can use to access the mysterious, beautiful, and incredible treasures of their own inner worlds.

We are at a significant period in human history. The rate of discovery in the sciences outpaces our ability to keep up with the amount of information generated. It is very telling that over the short course of eighteen months it took to write this book, there were two significant discoveries in the brain sciences that necessitated my editing portions of the manuscript.

At no time in recorded history have we acquired so much knowledge in so short a time.

Knowledge is power. But knowledge carries with it a shadow side. For without wisdom to use that knowledge in life affirming ways, we may very well destroy ourselves.

The ancient Chinese ideogram for transformation consists of two words — danger and opportunity. All transformations involve change whether it be the transformation of biochemistry into mind or the transformation of a society.

In the ever growing complex world in which we live, we must transcend our old ways of viewing and doing things. We must discover new ways to learn and to work. This is as true on an economic level as it is on a personal one. Those societies that educate themselves to be the most creative and motivated may well be those which flourish in the coming century. And on a personal level, access to our greater potential gifts us with new levels of fulfillment and success.

It is my experience that altered states of awareness can assist us to reach beyond our current views of ourselves, and to discover a rich and powerful inner world. The insights, creativity, and sensitivity born from our own inner exploration can help us to wrestle free opportunities for greater life and growth.

This is the value I see in learning how to access one's deeper consciousness. And that is why I wrote this book.

I wish to thank my publisher, Larry Moen, for his foresight and vision to publish such a book as this. I wish to thank my editor, Ellie Sommer, for her helpful comments. I would also like to thank Bob and Judy Bennett for their help in preparing the manuscript. Finally, I would like to thank all those whose lives and stories contributed to this book and to my work.

My final words are directly to you the reader: Although we may never meet, and although I can reach out to you only with words, I trust and believe in your greatness. For no matter where we are in our attainments, we can always go further. I hope the following pages entertain, educate, and enlighten you. May they persuade you to take the Great Journey.

C. Thomas Kenyon
Orcas Island
Washington State
March 1994

CHAPTER ONE

Pegasus

"The most beautiful thing we can experience is the mysterious."
– Albert Einstein

A few years ago, a woman in her late forties was referred to me by a clinical social worker.

When Margo walked into my office, she struck me as a woman who was used to getting what she wanted. Her words were exact, like her movements, which resembled the cut of a diamond.

As she talked with me in the late afternoon light of November, I noticed an awful anguish in her voice. She had just received an offer to fly overseas to do a story. The old journalist in her was ready to pack her bags and be gone, but her body, seemingly with a mind of its own, was dying.

The most recent of her X-rays had revealed that her cancer

was spreading, and her T-cell counts elevating by the day.

It hurt to move; she was in constant pain.

As she told me of her past, I noticed that her face lightened when she spoke about Sedona, Arizona. As we talked, she revealed that one of her dreams was to live there, out on the desert.

Casually reaching over to the stereo system in my office, I asked her to close her eyes, and to just "float in the music for awhile."

The music I had chosen was especially written with spacious silences between the lush phrases. Choosing my words most carefully, I invited her to have a fantasy.

I asked her to imagine that she was in Sedona. Looking across the desert floor, she would be drawn to a large boulder. When she found it, she was to nod her head. In a moment, she signaled that she was there.

I then asked her to feel and sense the "healing energy" coming from the geological formation. As she internally experienced the feelings coming to her from the imaginary rock, she began to relax. In fact, her entire posture changed as the imaging process continued. Soon, she was smiling and breathing easily.

Again, choosing my words most carefully, I guided her deeper into the fantasy, telling her to bring the "energy" from the rock up into her spine where the cancer was most rampant. For the next several minutes, I invited her to bathe in this "healing energy."

When she opened her eyes, there was a single tear, which she deftly patted with a lace handkerchief. Looking up, she glanced about the room in a perplexing way.

"It's gone!" she said.

"What's gone?" I asked.

"The pain... what did you do?"

Indeed! On the surface of things it looked as if all she did was listen to some "pretty music" while I told her a story about the desert. And yet, what we had done was activate the "deeper" abilities of the brain/mind through a precise choice of music and language.

One of the abilities of the brain/mind is self-healing, and, through the agency of endorphins, it is possible to reduce or eliminate physical pain, as with Margo. Endorphins are a class of brain chemicals sometimes referred to as the "body's natural opiates." They both reduce the perception of pain and increase the experience of pleasure. They are powerful substances and under the right conditions the brain can be coaxed into producing them in large quantities.

It would have been nice to report that Margo's pain never returned, but it did. And Margo died three years later from her disease. But during that time she was able to travel and do the things she always wanted to do: swim with the dolphins, re-visit Sedona. Her doctors kept saying she was a miracle. And through the whole thing, to use Margo's own words, "I have come to know myself much more deeply."

That is one of the ideas behind this book.

On the portals to many of the ancient Greek Mystery Schools, there were inscriptions: "Know Thyself." It implied that greater accomplishments would be attained through greater knowledge and wisdom.

As we enter the twenty-first century, our understanding of the brain/mind is accelerating at an incredible rate. This understanding is birthing radical and new techniques which allow persons to greatly accelerate their performance and abilities.

In these pages, you will discover how you can alter your own brain state, thereby releasing potentials beyond your imagination.

- You will learn how your "mind" speaks to your body, and how to use this knowledge to reduce stress and improve health.
- You will discover how to create "healing" experiences within your own mind thereby improving the physical functioning of your body.
- You will learn how to use your almost unlimited abilities to accelerate learning and process information.
- And through the techniques we will discuss, you will learn how to more fully experience the depth and the richness of life.

It is a very exciting time in the field of human potential; for at no other time in modern history have we glimpsed so clearly the relationships between "the mind" and the body. And at no other time have the technologies that can make possible a richer and fuller life been made more available to the masses.

It is my intention, in these pages, to show you how to greatly improve your mental functioning and, to use a metaphor, reach the lofty heights of your own Pegasus.

Pegasus, according to ancient Greek mythology, was created from the blood of Medusa, the snake-haired Gorgon, and with a kick of his hoof he opened the spring of Hippocrene.

The spring flowed from out of Mount Helicon, reputed by the Greeks to be the source of poetic inspiration.

Truly "the mind" has the power to open the springs of inspiration. And neurophysiology has clearly demonstrated that "the mind" is created from blood — in that the flow of oxygen and nutrient rich blood into the brain allows the phenomenon of mind to take place. Although I wonder if the ancient Greeks had this in mind, parts of the brain resemble snakes coiled in and about themselves.

You may have noticed that I put "the mind" in quotes. That

is because, from a neurophysiological standpoint, there is no such thing as "the mind."

To use Karl Pribram's analysis, "the mind" is a process, not a thing. It is a process that runs parallel to physical processes in the brain. You can, for instance, have a brain without a mind, as in a cadaver, but you cannot have a mind without a brain — at least not in the way we normally think of mental/emotional experience.

This is not to say that there is not some aspect of consciousness independent of brain neurophysiology. Indeed some anecdotal research on Near Death Experiences (NDEs) would indicate that consciousness does transcend the mind as well as the physiological processes within the brain itself. Most of our reports from persons encountering NDEs come from medical emergencies. In a typical NDE, the patient has suddenly died, either during an operation or an accident. His brain activity has ceased, making him clinically dead, and according to prevailing neurophysiology there should be no experience, just the darkness of death. However, quite the contrary seems to be the case. These persons report an almost universal experience of floating "up and out of their bodies," as if they were looking down at themselves. They could see everyone around them and hear conversations. Many of their reports are uncannily accurate. How did they perceive such things without brain activity? These are basically unanswerable questions at the present moment. But let them remind us of the limitations of our grandest schemes and theories for explaining human experience. Still, for most of us most of the time, our experiences of ourselves and of the world seem to parallel neurophysiological activity within the brain itself.

Let's take the Pegasus myth a little further. Pegasus, for all its winged glory, is first a horse. Its wings sprout forth from the sides of an earthly beast. And even though it could soar through the heavens, it was made from the very stuff of terra firma.

How eloquent a metaphor for the interrelationships between the brain and the mind. For, as we now know from brain research, every thought and feeling shimmers in the physical structures of the brain itself.

Even as you read these words, there are biochemical and electrical patterns in the brain. These patterns are "the signature," if you will, of the corresponding experiences in your mind. In other words, as the Pegasus of the mind takes to the wing, the horse is on earth plowing the fields. There is some very significant brain research which indicates that new neurological connections may be "furrowed" in the tissue of the brain itself as the result of powerful or continuous thought patterns.

To explain how the mind and brain interact, we will take a short detour, not through the world of man, but through the world of the amoeba.

What, you might ask, does the amoeba have to do with me? A lot.

CHAPTER TWO

Amoebas, Neurons, and Other Galactic Oddities

"An invitation is offered to cross a bridge as vast as the infinite space surrounding us and as small as the width of a neuron's membrane. This is a journey into unknown territory, a voyage into the mind. To know the mind is to know the universe."
— *Fred Alan Wolf,* Star Wave

A moebas are fascinating little creatures. Although unicellular (only one cell), they can move through the watery depths of a single drop of water.

You may recall from biology classes that these critters are microscopic and can't be seen with the "naked eye." There can be hundreds of them in a single drop of water. They cluster and forage for food in ponds and streams and swim unnoticed in small stagnant puddles at shopping malls.

With their pseudopods they slide through their tiny world like mammoth monsters engulfing everything (edible) in sight.

Now, what is fascinating about them is that they have no real nervous systems. They are, after all, just one cell. But they can detect light and darkness, warmth and cold, and can discern something edible from something toxic.

Their ability to move puts them into the class of animals, the same class held by African elephants and man. But although amoebas live and die, they do not have dreams and do not make poetry or music, at least not the way we perceive these things.

Amoebas have many things to teach us. One of them is that even one tiny cell can sensate (feel) and make "decisions" about its environment. These decisions are obviously unlike those of yours and mine. Amoebas do not have brains. However, in the infinitesimally small world of their bodies, there are sophisticated chemical and electrical processes taking place. When coordinated, they spell life for one of earth's tiniest creatures. And through these chemical processes, the amoeba is able to move through and experience its world.

From amoebas we jump into the body of man with its multitudinous number of cells. Think of yourself as a convention of about a trillion amoebas, and you have some idea of the intricate balance that is needed to keep you alive.

As you look to the higher order of animals, say from the crustaceans (lobsters and crayfish) to birds and dogs, on up to man and dolphins, you see increasingly complex assemblages of nervous systems.

The amoeba only needs a few parts of its one-celled body to coordinate its movements and other activities. But in a collection of cells like you or me, it takes a more complicated arrangement to coordinate things, which is the job of the central nervous system. (In man, this consists of the brain, brain stem, and spinal cord.)

In the very complex intercellular relationships that make up your body, the cells have specialized into a set of functions. For instance, the cells of your pancreas (one of the "ductless" or endocrine glands) secrete insulin while the cells in the heart beat out the rhythm of your life. Although the heart cells do their job fabulously well, they could not begin to secrete insulin, nor could the pancreas pump blood. Each type of cell has its unique place in this great collection of cells we call the body.

In the human nervous system, there are an important group of specialized cells called neurons.

Like the amoebas, neurons are fascinating one-celled entities. They don't move around, so, unlike amoebas, they are not classed as animals. However, very few animals could live without them. The more complex an animal becomes, the more dependent it is on these neuronal interconnections or networks.

Without the cooperation and networking of these microscopic cells, for instance, you could not read this book, nor hold it in your hands.

Neurons have several different parts, the most important being the soma body, the axon, and the dendrites.

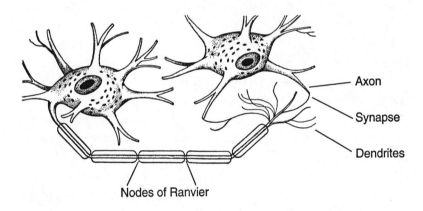

Figure 1

As you can see from the diagram, the axon sends the signal or nerve impulse out to the dendrites, which send it on to the soma body (the central processor if you like that analogy), which in turn, sends it on to the axon, and so forth. Those little gaps between the axons and dendrites are called synapses, and the signal has to literally jump this tiny gap each time it goes to another nerve cell. I will explain this in more detail later, but for now, I'd like you to think of the nervous system in a whole different way.

Instead of thinking about the parts that make up the nervous system, I'd like you to consider its main task, which is the collection and processing of information.

In - form - ation. The Latin stem from which our word inform emerges is *informare* which means to form or shape. Thus the word *information* implies a process of formation or shaping.

Another way to put this is that the meaning is in the form or structure.

Let me give you an example:

"An you me give let example."

The weird sentence above has the exact same words as the sentence before it, but it doesn't make sense.

The order of the words (or form) is crucial to the meaning. When the words are "out of order" or in the "wrong form" there is chaos or no meaning.

This is called syntax. Syntax is the correct ordering of words (which are symbols) to make meaning.

Strictly speaking, syntax refers only to words, but I would like to expand the idea to include something I call "biological syntax." Within every cell of your body is something called DNA (Deoxyribonucleic Acid). DNA is tucked away in the nucleus or center of most cells in the form of a double spiral or helix, and it is responsible for every physical attribute, as well as many of the abilities, you possess.

The DNA spiral is made up of tiny molecular building blocks called nucleotides. Think of them as teeny tiny Legos or Tinker Toys.

Now what is important about these nucleotides is their order, or the way they are laid out on the helix, the form, if you will. One sequence may give you green eyes, another blue, or another two heads. We call animals with two heads mutations. And usually they are caused by a mistake in the sequence of nucleotides. Thus, these tiny molecules spell out our "biological syntax." When they are in order they create life and perhaps beauty. When a syntactical error has occurred, there is chaos, and the result may be a mutation or even death.

The DNA determines the structure or form of an organism's nervous system. And it is the structure of an animal's nervous system that defines what is possible and what is not.

Now let's talk about "the mind" for a moment. You will never be able to fully experience the world of the amoeba, nor will the amoeba ever be able to experience your world as you experience it.

You may both be in the parking lot of the local mall, but the amoeba is swimming around in one of those little puddles, while you are carrying bags to your car. An amoeba will never go Christmas shopping, nor would it ever understand the meaning of it.

The reason for this, as we shall soon explore more fully, lies in the form or structure of the nervous system (which is, remember, dictated by the DNA).

Take my dog Merlin, for instance. Merlin has a much more sophisticated nervous system than an amoeba. Merlin weighs around 160 pounds and is a genetic smorgasbord, part Great Dane, part Saint Bernard, and part Bloodhound.

Now, as any anatomist will tell you, Merlin's brain is vastly different from yours and mine. The number of neurological connections between cells in the neocortex (where we "think") is much smaller in Merlin than in a human.

Merlin will never understand Shakespeare, his vocabulary list is limited to maybe twenty-five words, and God help me if he ever had to do the grocery shopping.

But if I am sad, Merlin is always there wagging his tail. On our evening walks, he sniffs the air with his hound dog snout and smells a world I hardly know exists. For, you see, if you look at a dog's brain, the olfactory (smell) areas are more developed than in man. Merlin also hears better than I do. He knows that someone is coming near the house before anyone else.

I often think of the world as a symphony of vibrations, some of which we see and hear and taste, and some which we feel and smell. Merlin is better at some of these than I am, and in this sense, his world is richer.

But Merlin will never read a book. And as I sit at my desk typing these words into the computer, he is oblivious to their meaning. He seems to just be waiting patiently for our evening walk through the trees and the shrubs.

Merlin's world is defined and limited by the form of his nervous system, as is mine, as is yours.

This might be a depressing thought except that we know from research that we are only using a small percentage of our actual mental abilities. The vastness of our unclaimed potential lies waiting before us.

It is truly amazing, when you think of man's vast accomplishments, to realize that the meter of a sonnet, a map of the galaxy, and the skill of a surgeon's knife are all made possible by the most sophisticated array of those tiny cells — the neurons.

And to understand them, I would like to bring us back to the amoebas.

One way to look at the life of an amoeba, or the life of any creature for that matter is as information.

Look at it like this: when the amoeba is out and about crawling its way through a drop of water, it is sensing its environment. As its pseudopods close in and around its potential supper, there are a myriad of sophisticated biochemical events taking place. The amoeba has bumped into something, and it is discerning whether or not it can eat it.

Without getting into complex biochemistry, (for our purposes we don't need to) we can describe the amoeba's sojourn in three words:

Reception - Integration - Transmission

The amoeba is able to *receive* information about its environment, in this case it has bumped into something that may be edible.

Through biochemical processes the amoeba is able to *integrate* this information about its potential dinner. It is able to get "a feel" for this thing it has encountered. The word "feel" may be a misplaced metaphor since the amoeba does not feel the way we feel, but you get the point, I hope.

Based on this "feel" for the object, the amoeba then *transmits* its "decision" to its ever wandering pseudopods. Or, perhaps, the "decision" originates in the pseudopods themselves. If the object is edible, the amoeba pulls the food into itself and digests it. If the object turns out to be inedible, the amoeba crawls around it.

In order to survive, all creatures, no matter how large or how small, must receive information about their environment. They must then integrate this information and make a decision. Finally, they must transmit this information within themselves and act.

Those animals, including both man and amoeba, which make the best decisions are the ones who survive.

In this context, intelligence (often an elusive and ephemeral concept) might be defined as the speed and accuracy by which neurons receive, integrate, and transmit information. (See Timothy Leary, Ph.D., *Info-Psychology*). These neurological decisions are pretty much out of our conscious awareness; they pass unnoticed from one neuron to the next, contributing to our experience of life.

Obviously the process of making decisions is much more complicated in man than in an amoeba. But, as we shall see, most of man's decisions, like those of the amoeba, are made automatically. Only a small portion of our decisions are actually conscious.

Now, my idea of a "decision" may be different from yours. You have, for instance, decided to read this book, and this was probably a conscious choice.

But as you read these pages, your body is making a lot of decisions you don't even know about. For instance, the respiratory center in your brain is monitoring your CO_2 levels. When the level of carbon dioxide rises past a genetically set point, you will spontaneously and automatically take a breath — without so much as a thought.

When you take that breath, you may or may not be aware of it. This is because the respiratory center is located in an area of your brain different from the thinking or language part. If you are totally engrossed in what you are reading, and oh, dear muses, make it so, you won't realize that you are breathing.

But if that respiratory center did not do its job, you would fall over and die from suffocation. Fortunately this is a rare occurrence.

The respiratory center is making some very sophisticated decisions, even if the syntax of its grammar is based on biochemical-electrical events and not words.

Most "decisions" within the brain and central nervous system are based on the neuron. Neurophysiologists used to think that the neuronal network was the sole information processor of the brain. Now, however, the picture is not so simple. It seems that hormones also may play a significant part in brain processing.

This new discovery of the hormonal or "wet" nature of the brain does not supplant the neuronal theory, rather it enhances our understanding of the process. Both types of processing (neuronal and hormonal) occur simultaneously. And I suspect that in the years to come we will uncover other types of brain processing not yet apparent to us.

For the purposes of mastering brain states here, we will focus exclusively on neuronal processing.

Earlier in this chapter, I laid out the basic structure of the nerve cell. In the brain's highly complex information net, the dendrites receive information, while the soma body integrates the information received by the dendrites. It is the axon that transmits information to other nerve cells.

This process of sending information along a nerve path is very complicated and involves both electrical and biochemical processes. Later, we will discuss neurotransmitters and their role in all of this.

But for now, the main point I want to get across is the idea of neural networking.

You see, one or two neurons by themselves cannot do much more than an amoeba. They would never be able to create the experience of reading a book. For that you need thousands of neurons interconnecting.

In fact, though you cannot sense it, there are thousands perhaps hundreds of thousands of these infinitesimally small neurons relaying their information to each other as you read. This relaying of information within the network of your brain is what is creating the experience in your mind of reading these words.

This is a key point that we will come to again and again — the brain and "the mind" are intimately connected. When you make changes in the structure of the brain or in the patterning of neurological connections, you are also changing experiences within the mind.

Until a few years ago it was a medical heresy to say that it might also be possible to affect the brain and the body through experiences within the mind.

But a growing body of research indicates that this is indeed the case. In subsequent chapters, we will discuss one of the major theories of how this happens. It is quite interesting, but before we can trek through the misty realms where the mind and body meet, we will need to cover some basic brain physiology.

I promise to keep it short and clear. I also promise that it will be worth the wait, for the views you see from Pegasus are all the more magnificent if you understand the horse.

The soaring achievements of the human mind are birthed out of matter. With every shift and nuance of experience in your mind, there is a corresponding change in the physical patterning of the brain.

And the brain is, for all of its sophistication, a bunch of fats, proteins, and water. It is born out of the earth itself, and when we die the trillions of molecules that make up our brains and bodies will return from whence they came.

The amoebas, ourselves, and the earth itself all share something in common. We don't often think of it in our day to day lives, but we are all birthed from the remnants of stars.

CHAPTER THREE

Pegasus and the Horse

"Think with the whole body."
– Taisen Deshimaru

There is danger in speaking of the brain/mind in terms of a metaphor. The danger is that we might become hypnotized by the metaphor, think it's real and forget that we invented it. The brain/mind, by definition, is far greater than anything it can create or use to describe itself.

The brain/mind is so vast and complex in its organization and function that it is virtually impossible to conceive of or describe it without deleting immense areas. But if we are to understand even some of its workings, we must do just that.

The scheme I am about to present is ludicrously simple given the complexity of the brain/mind system. However, it will serve our attempts to alter our brain state. And that is, after all, the intention of this book.

If you think of the brain as an information management system, many aspects of our mental and emotional experience become apparent.

For our purposes, we will divide the brain/mind system into four levels. Each of these levels is concerned with highly specific types of information.

For instance, level one is concerned with keeping our bodies alive. It couldn't care less about you reading or understanding this book. In fact it is neurologically unequipped to "think" at all. Thinking is confined to the third level (neocortex) of brain management.

Each level of the brain/mind system processes information unique to itself. And while all of the levels interconnect, they are not able to take over the information functions of each other.

Let me use a mechanical metaphor here to demonstrate my point. Recently our family went on a short vacation to Wilmington, North Carolina, where the large World War II battleship U.S.S. *Wilmington* is moored. Preserved by the citizens of North Carolina back in the 1950s, the huge battleship is now a national memorial. Every year, thousands of people roam over its decks and through its insides to get a sense of naval life during the Second World War.

The massive ship required more than two thousand men to run it. Deep in its bowels surrounded by steel and thousands of miles of cable were the ship's engines. This was the vessel's most crucial level. If it malfunctioned, the ship would sit dead in the water. The engine room was, to use our analogy, the first level of the ship's information management system. The men who manned the engine room never actually saw what was happening around the ship. They depended on other systems in the ship to inform them.

The second level of information management within the

battleship was concerned with support systems. This included the galley areas where food was prepared, the medical hospital, gunneries, and the hundreds of other tasks needed to keep the ship going. While this level of management had contact with the first level, it could never have taken over the job of running the engines.

The third level of information management within the ship was the bridge. The activities of the massive battleship were directed from here. It was from the bridge that you could most clearly see what was happening around you.

The fourth level of the ship's information management system was the captain. He made decisions that directly affected the lives and well-being of the crew and the safety of the ship.

I use this metaphor to point out that while each of the levels of the ship were interconnected, and in many ways interdependent, they were each concerned with unique types of information.

In the heat of battle, for instance, while the engine room hummed with activity to keep the ship afloat and moving, the galley areas in the second level were busy cooking meals for the crew, and the gunnery crews were firing salvos. While these two levels were not directly aware of each others' activities, all of the levels were needed for the optimal performance of the ship.

Looking at the brain's management of information as a whole, the similarities to our battleship analogy are clear.

In the diagram below, you will see the brain/mind system as viewed through levels of information management. The first three levels are followed by some unusual words in parenthesis. These terms, Reptilian, Paleomallian, and Neomammalian come from the work of Paul MacLean, M.D.

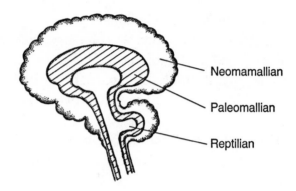

Neomamallian

Paleomallian

Reptilian

Figure 2

Dr. MacLean has conceived a system of the brain's organization in terms of its evolutionary development.

According to Dr. MacLean, one of the first brains to develop was that of the reptiles. This primitive brain conducts the most rudimentary of functions necessary for life. Our respiration is controlled from this level. This brain has been called, understandably, the Reptilian brain, and it correlates in our metaphor with the first level.

In the course of evolution, it appears that nature just made additions to the brain rather than redesign it over again. As we move from reptiles to mammals, we see a much more sophisticated brain that sits right on top of the older or Reptilian brain. This brain allowed animals to feel and have emotions. It also gave them more control of the environment. Dr. MacLean calls this brain the Paleomallian brain, and it correlates with our middle management analogy.

As we move to the higher mammals, including man, dolphins, and whales, we see the emergence of the vast neocortex that allows us to think, reason, and make language. This Neomammalian brain sits on top of our middle brain, which, in turn, sits on top of the primitive Reptilian brain. This last, and most recent brain, correlates with our upper management metaphor.

The final and fourth level of information management does not have a physical location. At least neuroscience has not found one yet. "The mind" correlates with our conscious awareness. Conscious awareness is a mental function that allows us to be, quite simply, aware of what is going on.

You are, for instance, aware that you are now reading a book. You may also be aware of your breathing. As I pointed out in Chapter 1, most of what happens is beyond our conscious awareness. We are, at any one time, only aware of a sliver of the goings-on within our brain/mind system. For instance, you are not aware of the biochemical and electrical activity within your primitive brain. However, without this activity you would die within minutes.

Our awareness of ourselves, or self-reflection, is a result of activity within the neocortex. With it we can make conscious decisions. These decisions may affect activity within the deeper areas of the brain through the actions we take. For instance, if I choose to swim underwater, the deeper structures within my brain will inhibit my breathing until I pop up for air.

Until quite recently it was thought that mental activity in the neocortex could not, in itself, affect the deeper structures in the brain. However, a growing body of evidence indicates that this is not true. Under certain conditions, thoughts, in and of themselves, can affect biochemical and electrical events in the deeper levels of the brain. This is revolutionary stuff, and in the end, I believe that it will turn our current views of human limitations upside down, or should I say right side up!

To deepen our understanding of the brain/mind system, let's take a look at the structures involved.

We begin our exploration with the first level of information management since it was the first to develop and is the most crucial to survival.

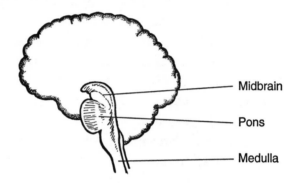

Figure 3

As the spinal cord moves up into the brain it swells into a structure called the medulla. The medulla is about one inch long and without it you could not live. It is responsible for breathing, the control of blood pressure, and heart beat to some extent. The medulla is also responsible for the reflexes of swallowing and vomiting.

Moving upwards from the medulla the swelling gets larger in an area called the pons. The pons comes from the Latin root meaning bridge. Through its wide range of fibers, it allows the third level (neocortex) to communicate with the cerebellum, located in the second level of management. The cerebellum, by the way, controls much of our ability to move.

Tucked above the pons is a structure called the midbrain. It is a type of relay station with primitive forms of seeing and hearing.

These three structures — medulla, pons, and midbrain – comprise the lower level of brain management. They are crucial to life, and they act automatically without conscious awareness.

This brings us to our next level of brain organization. The second level is concerned with emotion and many of the autonomic (or automatic) functions of our body. There are several key structures within this system.

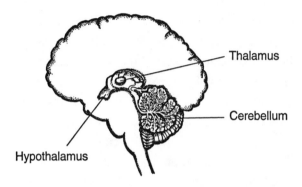

Thalamus

Cerebellum

Hypothalamus

Figure 4

The relaying of information both within and through the second level is accomplished by a group of cells called the thalamus.

The thalamus is a kind of neurological relay station that sends all sensory information, except for smell, to the third level of management located in the great overarching cerebral hemispheres of the neocortex.

Tucked underneath the thalamus is a structure called the hypothalamus. It is the control center for such things as food intake, sexual activity, endocrine levels, water retention, and the autonomic nervous system. It is this structure that connects together all of the other levels of information management. The hypothalamus is in direct communication with all of the systems and organs of the body via a complex neurological network.

Encircling the hypothalamus and thalamus is another very important structure. Called the limbic system, this area is involved with feelings, and it coordinates emotions with activities within the hypothalamus, such as the release of hormones. The limbic system is one of the key managers within the second level, and not only is our emotional well-being dependent upon it, but evidently much of our learning as well.

Located towards the back of the head there is a structure called the cerebellum. It is responsible for executing controlled and coordinated movement, and without it you could not walk.

The cerebellum has the ability to manage impressive levels of movement-related information. Witness the graceful movements of a dancer or the precise actions of an athlete and you will better appreciate the cerebellum's abilities.

These four areas then, thalamus, hypothalamus, limbic system, and cerebellum are responsible for the second level functions.

There is something very important within the second level of information management. It is only at this level of the brain/mind system that we feel. Thus it is from here that we are able to love and to care for others. It is also here that we feel anger, hatred, and jealousy. Lower management, (Reptilian), is incapable of creating emotional experiences as we usually think of them.

I believe that one of the crucial challenges facing twenty-first century man is how to integrate feeling with thinking. Anatomically, they are capable of operating independently of each other.

The ability to think and act without connection to our feeling self is not, in my opinion, a positive development. It leads to all kinds of personal and social problems.

This is why someone can kill another human being without remorse. It is one of the reasons that weapons of mass destruction proliferate. And it is how, as a civilization, we have raped and pillaged the planet and its indigenous cultures.

Corporate officers perched in the dazzling height of sky scrapers often make intellectual decisions that affect thousands, if not millions of individuals. Rarely, if ever, is any attention given to the emotional impact of these decisions. The "bottom line" is a purely mental concept. It has no bearing on real people or how they might be affected.

Our culture has made a demi-god out of reason and the intellect. Feeling has been relegated to a submissive position, and I believe we are paying a terrible price for this imbalance. The rise in drug and alcohol addictions as well as the increase in violent crimes all point to how cut off we are from our feeling selves.

Until we recognize and accept our feeling selves with all of their rawness and irrationality, we will be imprisoned by and under the influence of our emotions. We cannot bypass them any longer, not as a culture and not as individuals.

But let's leave philosophy and return to our brain architecture. Overarching the middle level of brain management and folding in on itself, looking much like a walnut, is the neocortex. The neocortex is, as I said earlier, where we think, reason, plan, and dream. It is also where we make language. Your ability to understand the words on these pages is a result of neurological activity within the neocortex.

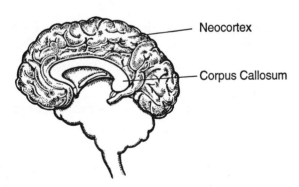

Figure 5

If by some terrible accident your neocortex were taken away, you would hardly be considered human. You would not be able to think or plan. The ability to plan, to conceive of the future, is a function of the frontal area of the cerebral cortex. What we cherish as very human experiences would be ripped away from you. You would no longer recognize the faces of those you love, nor could you understand what they were saying. You would still be alive, for the first and second levels of management would continue to do their jobs. But your essential humanity would be gone.

The frontal area of the brain, by the way, does not fully develop in humans until around seven years of age, which is why young children cannot imagine waiting for something in the future. Everything must be now. And if it is not happening now, they cannot conceive of it.

I saw this graphically demonstrated the other day in the supermarket. A young and harried mother was desperately trying to reason with her toddler about the package of ice cream bars he had put into the grocery cart. She wanted him to wait until after dinner to eat one. He wanted to eat it then.

They were deadlocked in that most ancient of human struggles, the one between a parent's will and that of his or her child.

As the mother became more rational, calmly explaining the basis for her decision, the child became more irrational screaming at the top of his lungs — "NOW!"

Finally overcome with her own irrational urges, the mother threw the box of ice cream bars back into the freezer section and stormed out of the store dragging her frenzied and sobbing son.

Understanding about the lack of development in her child's frontal area would not have helped the distressed little person. But, it might have helped the parent realize that her cute two-year-old-turned-monster-from-hell was not just being obstinate for the sake of being obstinate.

As we grow and mature from conception onward, the neurological connections within the neocortex get more involved and sophisticated in their networking. The neocortex finally emerges as the most vastly complicated area of the brain. We will not even begin to attempt to discuss these many and divergent areas. Rather, we will focus only on those few areas that have a direct concern for us in our attempts to master the brain/mind system.

One way of viewing the third level is in the terms of management styles. Each style of dealing with challenges and problems has its own set of positives and its own set of limitations.

For whatever reason, the third level (neocortex), has evolved into two separate yet anatomically similar parts. It's as if someone drew a line down the middle of the brain and created two mirror images.

I am, of course, referring to the right and left cerebral hemispheres. Although wide areas of the neocortex are involved in the processing of information it seems that the left and right sides of the brain have different biases in regard to incoming information.

Think of the left and right hemispheres as a "management team," and you may be better able to understand how these two separate, yet connected systems work. One of the crucial elements in any successful management team is communication. This is accomplished by our "management team" through the corpus callosum, a thick band of fibers that connect the left and right hemispheres. It is through this bundle of nerves that the two hemispheres can "talk" to each other.

So how do these two different parts manage information?

The hemisphere controlling speech and language is often called the dominant hemisphere. This dominant hemisphere is usually the left, although some people are reversed. How one hemisphere becomes dominant is not fully understood, although it is thought that heredity, early experiences, and education have a large role to play in it.

The dominant hemisphere is, for the most part, logical, sequential, concerned with the details; being highly verbal it is always describing things, noting differences, and making up categories or boxes to put everything into. It is your typical managerial type — precise and logical in everything it does.

The non-dominant hemisphere is primarily concerned with different types of information from the dominant hemisphere. Unlike its neighbor, the non-dominant hemisphere does not look so much at the details of things as at the "big picture." It has a tendency to see things as interrelated rather than opposed. It, unlike the dominant hemisphere, is quite comfortable in the realm of paradox, where things do not logically make sense, but are, nevertheless, true. There are other differences as well.

Positron emission tomography (PET) scans of the brain show a marked difference, for instance, between the two cerebral hemispheres. PET scans record an increase in glucose consumption in different areas of the brain through a process that measures specific types of emissions. Since glucose is the brain's primary energy source it can be concluded that those areas that show increases in glucose consumption are more active than other areas.

If a person listens to spoken language there will be in most cases, an increase of neuronal activity in the left hemisphere. When those same subjects, however, listen passively to music, most of them will show an increase in activity on the right side.

The non-dominant hemisphere is also often described as "intuitive." Unlike the dominant hemisphere which will analyze a situation in detail and then make a logical assumption, the non-dominant hemisphere looks at the whole situation as a process and then gets a "hunch" as to the right course of action.

There is another very significant difference between the dominant and non-dominant hemispheres. How many times have you or someone you know experienced a strong feeling about something, but were unable to explain it or put it into words? The reason for this is that the non-dominant hemisphere is not verbal. It does not talk.

In such an instance, the non-dominant hemisphere is sensing something in the patterning of information. This something is a characteristic that the dominant hemisphere is not prone to notice due to its "managerial style," which is analytical and sequential. Something out of sequence can slip by the dominant hemisphere.

Actually, the labeling of the two cerebral hemispheres as dominant or non-dominant is biased. It is biased towards the skills of language and logic, both of which are highly revered in our culture.

There are ways to bring the two hemispheres together so that they are both working in harmony. This greatly increases problem solving abilities; creativity; and, it seems, certain intelligence factors as well. I will discuss this in detail, and show you how to improve your abilities of information management later in this book.

In actuality, the view I have just presented may be obsolete in the near future since recent research indicates that vast areas of the brain are involved in the processing of information. Our current concept of left brain/right brain may not accurately describe the situation. Nevertheless, whatever the mechanism is there are different operational styles when it comes to the processing of information.

In this regard, you will find that the non-dominant styles of processing offer a unique perspective.

But for now I'd like to turn our attention to the last level of our brain/mind system. As I mentioned earlier, our "minds" do not have a physical location. "The mind" is non-physical because it is a mental function. Through it we are aware of ourselves and can make "conscious" decisions.

It is now believed by a growing number of researchers and theorists that our mind interacts with the brain and body via the hypothalamus (second level).

In his book, Th*e Psychobiology of Mind/Body Healing*, Ernst Rossi, M.D., has presented a model of how the brain and mind interrelate through a process called "transduction." To explain transduction, I will have to take us back to my fifth grade class.

As I recall, it was a day in early spring and Mr. Keogh, my fifth grade science teacher, had just lit a gas burner. Above the flame a glass beaker, filled with water, sat silent and still.

Within minutes, however, the water had turned to a fervent turmoil. Bubbles hissed to the surface and white steam poured into the classroom. The water had turned to the boiling point.

Slipping a rubber tube over the neck of the beaker, Mr. Keogh inserted the other end into the valve of what later turned out to be a small steam turbine. A few moments latter, the turbine started to spin and a tiny light bulb next to the brass contraption lit up.

"What have we just done?" asked Mr. Keogh.

Derek Rankin, the whiz kid, raised his hand.

"Yes Derek?" Mr. Keogh asked.

"You created energy," said Derek.

"Wrong..." said Mr. Keogh. "We did not create energy. Energy cannot be created or destroyed. Anyone else?" Mr. Keogh glanced about the room.

No one said a thing.

Mr. Keogh turned and faced the blackboard, a piece

of chalk poised in hand.

Just at that moment a jet fighter made of notebook paper broke the imaginary sound barrier and sailed right over my head. The pilotless jet dropped and hit the back of Derek's chair.

The plane fell with a soundless thud onto my opened science book. I saw writing folded over into one of the wings.

Opening it I read the words- "WRONG DIMBO... KEOGH CHANGED ENERGY FROM ONE FORM INTO ANOTHER... THE LONE RANGER."

That was Bobby... aloof, mysterious, and always playing dumb when any of the teachers called on him.

I looked to the back of the room where he always sat.

I folded the airplane back into its original form, and sailed it back to Bobby's waiting hands.

Unfortunately, Mr. Keogh had just turned around and saw me piloting the paper jet.

"Tommy Kenyon... perhaps you'd like to tell us what I just did."

I swallowed hard and then remembered the words Bobby had scrawled on the wings of his imaginary jet.

"You changed energy from one form to another."

Mr. Keogh got the oddest expression on his face, looked down at his book, and mumbled "Correct."

From that day on, and for the rest of the school year, Bobby and I had a kind of odd friendship. The last day of school, before he moved to Colorado with his mom, he handed me a paper airplane. On one of the wings he had written the words "Energy changes form... the Lone Ranger rides again."

Everything is energy. We know, for instance, through particle physics, that the book in your hands has tremendous potential energy. You could burn it and release a certain amount of energy, but if you split the atoms of which it is made, you would have released an unbelievable amount of energy. Atomic power is generated from very small amounts of matter.

Energy and matter are always changing forms. A thousand years from now there is a very good chance that this book will be ash or even dissolved into trillions of subatomic particles.

Energy is also always changing form within our nervous system. Your very act of reading is a process involving thousands upon thousands of energy transformations.

To recap the short anatomy lesson from Chapter 2, the human nerve cell, or neuron, has four main parts. The dendrites receive incoming information and pass it on to the main cell body or soma. The soma body then integrates the information and sends it on to the axons, which send the information to the waiting dendrites of other nerve cells. Between the axons and dendrites there is a small gap or space called a synapse.

This information that is passed along the network of neurons takes the form of chemical and electrical energy. At the axon and dendrite ends of the nerve cell, the energy takes the form of chemical processes, while in the rest of the cell the process is chemical/electric. Let's take a closer look at what's happening here.

The simplest way to conceive of it is in terms of a three dimensional puzzle. A puzzle has many different pieces, and each piece fits exactly into only one spot. When you put all of the pieces into the right spots, the puzzle is completed.

In the biochemical world of neurons, these puzzle pieces are called neurotransmitters. They are highly specific molecules and each has a unique shape. When the end of an axon is stimulated due to electrical activity within the cell, it releases some of these biochemical puzzle pieces (neurotransmitters). These neurotransmitters then literally jump across the synapse to the waiting neurotransmitter sites at the tip of the waiting dendrites. Once the biochemical pieces of the puzzle fit into the right spots, an electrical activity is set off in the cell, and it travels down the length of the dendrite into the soma body. If all of the conditions are met, this electrical surge is then passed onto the axon where the process is started all over again.

When the chemical activity at the neurotransmitter sites of a dendrite sets off an electrical surge within the cell, this is transduction. And when this same electric potential travels into the axon and generates chemical activity at its tip, it is also transduction. Every sensation and thought involves thousands upon thousands of such transductions. (See diagram below).

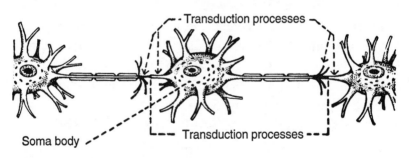

Figure 6

One of the side effects of these transduction processes within brain cells is that they emit electrical fields. When enough cells participate in a transduction process (i.e. when they get stimulated), it is possible to measure their combined electrical activity. This electrical activity has very characteristic patterns. These patterns, or brain waves, are a key and important concept in the next chapter.

At this point in time, there is no consensus on exactly how changes in mental and emotional experience transduce into physical processes within the brain and body. However, based on Dr. Rossi's model, it would seem that neurological activity within the brain, specifically the neocortex, gets routed into the hypothalamus where it is "transduced" into mental phenomena.

Likewise, mental phenomena, such as thinking, are routed "back into" the hypothalamus where they are transduced into the biochemical and electrical language of the brain.

Thus, within this model, the hypothalamus is a kind of two-way revolving door. It may open out into the ephemeral world of "the mind" or into the biochemical and electrical world of the brain.

Undoubtedly as research in this area continues, we will begin to more fully understand how mind and brain interrelate. Even though we may not yet fully understand the intricacies of this interconnectedness, we can take advantage of the process.

All this information tells us that under certain conditions, it is possible to radically affect organs and systems in the body and systems within the brain that we previously thought could not be reached through conscious volition.

In other words, you can accelerate healing in yourself by making changes in your mental and emotional experience. You can increase your intelligence, decrease stress, and improve both mental and physical performance by making changes in your mind.

There are several keys that will allow you to open the door to these new possibilities. One of these keys is based in the electro-magnetic fields of your neurons. It sounds complicated, but it is really quite simple.

The term is "brain state." It is what this book is about, and all of our talk, so far, has been to get to this point.

To introduce our discussion of brain states, I would like to start with a remarkable person named Angela.

CHAPTER FOUR

Brain States

> *"The ultimate creative capacity of the brain*
> *may be, for all practical purposes, infinite."*
> — *George Leonard*

Angela came to see me because she was terrified of tests. A bright and beautiful senior in high school, she never came up to her potential. No matter how hard she studied, no matter how much she knew, when it came exam time, Angela froze up.

After spending the first thirty minutes with her, tracking the history of her disabling fear, I asked her to close her eyes.

"Relax into your exhale," I said, as I reached over and turned on some soft slow music. And let each exhale be more relaxed than the one before it."

As Angela settled down, I asked her to remember a time when she felt very relaxed. She nodded her head and her breathing became softer, more relaxed. Angela had changed her brain state.

By working in this relaxed brain state, I was able to help Angela erase her fear of exams.

A week later her father called me excitedly. "I don't know what you did, but Angela is a different person. It's like she blossomed overnight. She's more confident, and she's not afraid of taking tests anymore!"

The benefit of changing brain states is not limited to education either. It can have profound medical benefits.

Larry Dossey, M.D., recounts an experience with a patient early in his residency that changed the course of his work in medicine. An elderly man had not been responding to treatment. Nothing from the arsenal of modern medicine seemed to be working. The man was, in fact, dying.

In a desperate attempt to save the man's life, Dr. Dossey struck upon a bold plan. It had nothing to do with allopathic medicine. It had never been taught in medical school. But in the face of death the young physician had nothing to lose.

He took the man aside and told him that the next day that he would heal him through an ancient shamanic ritual. The man nodded in agreement. When the next day arrived, Dr. Dossey took the man into his office and guided him into a deep hypnotic trance. Through an elaborate set of rituals, Dr. Dossey impressed upon the man that he had been completely healed.

The next day, upon arriving at the hospital, Dr. Dossey discovered that the man's condition had reversed itself. The man completely recovered from his strange affliction.

Larry Dossey had succeeded in altering the man's brain state. And by so doing, he was able to affect a radical and rapid improvement in his condition.

This, too, is the potential power of brain states.

As we progress, I will show you how to alter your own brain state to improve the quality your life and performance.

However before we jump into the mysteries of the brain and mind, let's backtrack a moment, and take a look at the humble neuron.

Each time a nerve cell is stimulated, it transduces energy. The biochemical reactions at the tips of the dendrites fire off electrical activity in the rest of the cell. As we noted in the last chapter, neurons emit electromagnetic fields when they are stimulated. And if enough neurons fire off simultaneously, there is an electrical surge in the brain. This sudden burst of electrical energy can be detected and measured.

The device to measure such brain activity is called an Electroencephalogram, or EEG. The resulting measurements are called brain waves.

At any given moment of brain stimulation, there are hundreds, perhaps thousands, of different energy states occurring. Some of these are electrical as detected by EEG measurements. Others are biochemical or magnetic, and most likely include states we don't even know about yet. Every thought and feeling has a corresponding brain state or electrical and biochemical profile.

Our current level of technology does not allow us to measure all of the activities within the brain. And, if we are ever able to do such a thing, the mathematical task to understand and interpret such data will be unbelievable.

Fortunately, for our purpose of increased performance and mental ability we need only deal with those brain states measured by EEG. And from this point onward, this simplified definition of brain states is what we will refer to.

Brain states have been divided into roughly seven categories. There is some disagreement as to where one brain state ends and the other begins, but generally speaking, neurologists use the following schema:

Super High Beta	= 35 - 150 Hz
K- complex	= 33 - 35 Hz
High Beta	= 16 - 32 Hz
Beta	= 12 - 16 Hz
Alpha	= 8 - 12 Hz
Theta	= 4 - 8 Hz
Delta	= 0.5 - 4 Hz

The abbreviation (Hz) behind each of the numbers stands for Hertz, which is a way to measure the frequency of vibration. It is the same as a cycle per second. In other words, 1 Hertz (Hz) = 1 Cycles Per Second (cps).

It is not necessary to understand how these vibrations are measured in order to alter your brain state. Therefore, we are not going to discuss these basic concepts in electricity and vibration. However, if you are interested, you can turn to Appendix A for a discussion of this topic.

Starting at the lowest level of brain activity we encounter Delta which *begins* at 0.5 Hz and goes up to 4 Hz. This happens when there is the least amount of energy within the brain. When your EEG activity drops *below* 0.5 Hz, you are classified as brain dead.

Delta is the domain of sleep. In the lowest levels of Delta there are no mental images and no awareness of the physical body. Most people experience sleep in these Delta states. However, some, notably seasoned meditators, can experience an altogether different state. In such a deep "meditative state" the person is asleep, yet fully conscious. Such a person reports being aware of himself, not as a person or a body, but rather as a point of "still awareness." It is a very unusual state, and there is no word for it currently in our language.

Moving upward from Delta, we enter Theta. In Theta, the

neurons are transducing energy at a faster rate than Delta and the EEG measurements get more active. In Theta there can be visual images. Such images can seem very real, and in some of the lower Theta states there is little or no sense of the physical body. A person may experience his body as a field of energy or as if parts of his body are floating in the air, unconnected to other parts. The list of possible bodily "aberrations" in Theta is quite large. This is not to say that all people experience alterations in their sense of the body, just that such changes often occur in the deeper levels of Theta.

The internal experience one has during Theta activity seems to be the most prevalent perceived reality. External reality to a greater or lesser extent is simply not experienced.

Theta is the ideal state for some types of accelerated learning, self-programming and psycho-immunology (self-healing). In the course of this book, you will learn how to generate Theta activity and use this powerful state to your own advantage.

The next higher state, higher in terms of electrical frequency, is Alpha. Alpha has become fairly well understood thanks to biofeedback. In Alpha, unlike Theta and Delta, a person is aware of his or her body.

The body is relaxed, which is why Alpha training is so effective in stress management. By training a person to produce Alpha at will, he or she is able to greatly reduce the stresses in his or her life. It is neurophysiologically difficult for most people to experience states of agitation or stress in Alpha or Theta.

Alpha has also been documented to accelerate learning. Alpha enhanced learning techniques, such as the Lozanov method (sometimes called Superlearning), greatly accelerate the learning of foreign languages. The Alpha state, in general, reduces the stress around learning.

The next brain state is Beta. Beta is characterized by a high state of alertness. Our normal waking state is generated by such levels of Beta activity.

Next is High Beta, a state of even greater alertness. It also seems to be related to some states of anxiety.

As we enter 33Hz, the state is called K-complex, and usually occurs in short bursts. There is quite a bit of speculation about this frequency. Many feel that it is characteristic of the "ah-ha" experiences of high creativity.

Super-High Beta states are just now being explored by researchers. Part of the reason for this is mechanical. The old EEG machines, the type that used graph paper and ink pens, only went up to around 30-35Hz. It wasn't until the advent of more sophisticated machines that these higher brain frequencies were even recorded. One of the pre-eminent researchers in this area is Valerie Hunt, Ph.D. In her work, she has documented that the brain goes up to at least 150Hz.

Because this area of research into Super High Beta activity is so new, there have been no extensive controlled studies. Anecdotal reports from some researchers indicate that some of these Super High Beta states produce phenomena such as "out-of-body experiences," Kundalini releases (powerful energy flows up the central nervous system into the brain and out into the peripheral nervous system), and other dynamic psycho-spiritual states.

There is currently much work being done on the lower Beta frequencies and learning. Joel F. Lubar, Ph.D. and Judith Lubar, M.S., L.C.S.W., from the University of Tennessee, have discovered that persons with attention deficit disorder (ADD) are generally unable to generate Beta activity when trying to focus on a task.

ADD individuals find it difficult to stick with tasks, such as studying or following directions. They seem to "flit" like moths from one thing to another. ADD can range from mild symptoms, which simply annoy, to full blown symptoms such as disruptive behaviors, total inability to focus or follow directions, and confusion. It can be very difficult to manage, especially in children.

While one of the standard treatments for ADD is medication, the Lubars have uncovered another strategy. When they use EEG to train ADD persons to produce Beta activity, the ADD symptoms often decrease or disappear altogether. While this research is still tentative, it seems that with some persons, EEG training may be as or more effective than resorting to drugs.

As we learn more about the relationships between the brain and "the mind," I predict that we will see more such advances in a non-pharmacological or drug-free approach. This is not to say that appropriate medication is wrong, just that it may not always be needed.

There is something to be said for learning how to self-generate Beta activity in the brain as opposed to having something "done to you." In cases where an individual "takes charge" successfully, there is an increase in self-esteem and something called "locus of self control." Locus of self control refers to the sense that an individual has some control over his or her own experiences and behavior. Increasing such a sense of control has innumerable positive effects on personality and behavior.

As our understanding of brain states increases, an ever growing complex picture of brain activity emerges. Through computer imaging, it is now possible to view brain states in new ways. One such method uses a twenty-four channel EEG, which is then routed into a computer for analysis. In addition to standard EEG analysis, the computer also generates a color-coded map of the brain. This "neuromap" allows us to view brain activity in a remarkably new fashion.

The neuromaps, below, show some very interesting things.

To understand the different colored areas and what they mean, I will need to tell you how the neuromap is generated.

The subject wears a cap, very much like a swimmers cap. This cap has twenty-four different detectors, twelve on each side. These detectors pick up electrical activity within the area of the brain directly beneath them and then send these signals on to the computer where they are interpreted. The computer "knows" where each of these detectors is located.

In addition, each of the brain frequencies is given a color code. Beta activity is white; Alpha is blue, while Theta is green and Delta is black.

When the computer analyzes the data, it represents the frequency at each site as a color. Thus, the resulting neuromap is a color-coded picture of various brain states throughout the brain. When looking at a neuromap, you are looking down at the head. The front of the brain is up and the back of the brain is down. The left side of the brain is to your left; the right side of the brain is to your right.

Our sample below is in black and white, so the different frequency ranges are actually in shades of gray.

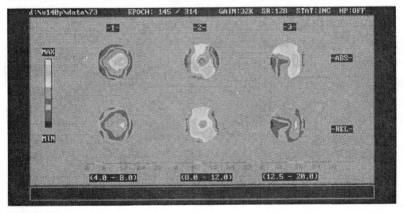

Figure 7

You will notice, in our sample neuromap, that there are many different brain states occurring throughout the brain simultaneously. To say that the brain has entered Alpha, for instance, is highly simplistic. Rarely, if ever, will you find the brain operating in a single brain frequency. Rather, there are numerous sites operating in different states. There can be a statistical increase in Alpha activity within the brain, that is, if you look at all the sites, you may find a general increase in Alpha. But you will not find Alpha activity at every site.

Research has shown that people have their own unique brain state profiles. In other words, no two people are exactly alike in how their brains process brain wave patterns.

Some people habitually "run" more Alpha activity than others, while some people seem to "run" more Beta activity. A lot can be gleaned from looking at neuromaps. Medical researchers can now pinpoint such behaviors as alcoholism, drug abuse, and depression along with a host of other brain dysfunctions simply by looking at the signatures of brain wave activity as indicated through neuromapping.

It is not in the scope of this book to discuss the subtleties of brain mapping. But I wanted to show you how brain states are spread throughout the brain and an example of how sound stimulation can radically affect brain processing. (The sample neuromap was recording the effects of specific sound patterns on the neocortex.) We will go into the effects of sound on the brain/ mind system in much greater detail in Chapter 13.

Next I want to show you how *you*, can change the electromagnetic patterning within your own brain. The ability to change your own brain state at will is a powerful resource. It will allow you to accelerate your brain/mind's hidden potential, and open worlds you may never have imagined existed.

CHAPTER FIVE

Changing Brain States

"Knowledge without experience is worse than useless."
— Anonymous Graffiti

S o far I have discussed how the brain/mind system works, how Brain States are created, and what these powerful resource states can do for you.

Now I am going to help you experience these various levels of mental power for yourself.

You will not need any fancy equipment to do this. You have everything you already need right between your ears.

If you have a cassette player, you will find information at the back of this book for a special tape called "Creative Imagining" which will make your journey of self-exploration easier and more entertaining. But you also can do these exercises without it.

My goal here is to help you reach a higher level of self-mastery than you now possess. This will be different for each of you, as we each have different abilities and levels of understanding that we bring to every new situation.

Think of me as a guide, pointing out important landmarks along the way. But it is up to you to take the journey.

I am reminded of one of those old Sufi stories rich with wisdom and paradox. The story concerns Nasrudin, one of the early Sufi saints. According to the story, the saint wandered from town to town on the back of his donkey asking each person he met the enigmatic question, "Where is my donkey?" What a stupid question. Wasn't he riding it all the time? Yes, and that is exactly the point of the story. He was riding it all the time. He had ridden it so long, in fact, he had totally forgotten about it.

As with most Sufi stories, there is a hidden meaning. The donkey is a symbol for the human nervous system. Nasrudin is the conscious mind. From this perspective the conscious mind (Nasrudin) rides on or is the result of the nervous system's activity (the donkey) but doesn't realize this. In other words, the conscious mind is too caught up in itself to realize that it is just an effect of something much deeper and more profound.

This is very much the case with us. Our experience of life, every thought and every feeling, is orchestrated in the biochemical sea of our brains and simultaneously in the heaven or hell of our minds. It is up to us to take the reins, if you will, of the donkey beneath us.

These exercises will teach you to do just that.

They will do this in a manner that may seem unusual. Instead of giving you the steps to do this, I will help you to discover it for yourself.

In our instant, push button world, some may find such a statement disquieting. But the type of mastery I am talking about (the mastery of your own brain/mind) requires a depth of understanding and experience. Such mastery can only come from direct experience.

Recall your childhood. Did anyone tell you how to walk or to talk? Of course not. You discovered how to do it by yourself. These two great accomplishments allowed you to fully enter the human family. The ability to stand upright against gravity and the ability to speak, to make and use language, are two very human traits. The neurological sophistication to accomplish these two tasks is quite awesome. Even more incredible, is that you achieved this without any directions. You just discovered how to do it.

This also is how you proceed here.

I will give you some hints, some ideas about the territory, and some suggestions on how to go about it. But you will discover how to do it yourself. And what is the "it" we are talking about? "It" is the process of discovery. The process of discovering how to master your own brain states. With this mastery, you will be able to tap into abilities and powers that will literally amaze you. These same abilities and powers can also change you, make you into a better person. The choice is yours. No one can make you do it.

It will not work to just read through this section.

You must do the exercises and discover through the power of your own experience how you can change your brain states.

In this chapter, you will be exploring how to change your brain states through several different means, such as through your breathing, through focused awareness, through body movements, and through something called internal awareness.

Let's first take a look at how "the mind" affects the brain and how breathing affects both of them. When I speak about "the mind," I am not talking about consciousness here.

When I say "mind," I am being very specific. I mean our day-to-day mental and emotional experiences. It is very clear from neurology that experiences in the mind are paralleled by physical processes in the brain.

The act of reading is the result of a sophisticated interplay between the occipital area of your brain (at the back of the head) which "sees" the letters and the language centers of the neocortex which interpret them.

If we were to damage the occipital area, say with a blow to the head, you would no longer "see" this book, much less the print on its pages. But if we damaged only the language areas, you would be able to see the letters; however, you would not be able to ascertain their meaning.

One of the things to understand here is that these two inti-mately interconnected systems, the brain and the mind, lie within two different dimensions.

You can touch, weigh, and measure the brain. You can quan-tify the neurological activity within the brain as well. But you cannot do this with the mind. This is because the mind is not in the physical dimension at all. You cannot touch it. You cannot weigh a thought or emotion. You may be able to measure the effects of that thought or emotion on the brain — that is you can follow its footprints (to use an analogy) as you might track a wildcat in the snow, but you will never trap the wildcat.

Neurology has established beyond the shadow of a doubt that changes in the brain create changes in mental and emotional experiences. The neurological sciences are now on the threshold of a radical idea — namely that changes within "the mind" can create changes within the brain.

But you see the problem here. Our very way of discussing the thing presupposes and reinforces the separation.

Think of the brain/mind as one interconnected system, and you will be coming much closer to the truth. Knowing how this elaborate system works gives you a tremendous amount of leverage. If you understand how the system works, you will be able to change mental and emotional experiences when you wish by altering your brain state.

Conceptualizing the brain/mind system as an information loop makes some of its workings more understandable. In the figure below, you see four aspects laid out along a circle, the implication being that these aspects are mutually interdependent and interactive.

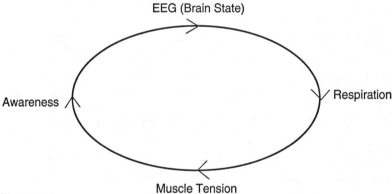

Figure 7

Brain state, as you may recall from Chapter 4, is the physical activity within the brain itself. This includes chemical and electrical activity, but for the purpose of altering mental and emotional experience we have focused on the electrical activity — specifically the EEG activity or brain waves.

As brain wave activity (or EEG) slows down, something happens to our respiration. Our breathing slows down and gets more relaxed.

We all experience this every day. Whenever you get relaxed, say take a nap or go to sleep, it happens to you. As you slip into relaxation, and as your muscles let go of tension, your breathing becomes more relaxed and shallow.

There is an intimate and important relationship between breathing and brain state. It is also a reciprocal relationship. The lowering of our brain state (i.e. transiting down to Theta and/or Delta, say for instance in sleep) slows down our breathing. However, we can also affect the system in the opposite direction. We can consciously change our breathing pattern and thereby alter our brain state.

We will go into this in more detail in just a bit, but for now I would like to move out of the physical dimension and into the nonphysical dimension of "the mind." This is at the left side of our information loop diagram in Figure 8.

Awareness has an immediate and direct effect on brain state. If you are driving your car and see a flashing light up ahead, your brain will immediately jump to a higher level of cortical activity. And it won't just be your neocortex that gets stimulated. Large areas of the deeper brain will also be active, pumping powerful hormones into the blood stream in order to stimulate alertness. Heart rate and blood pressure as well as respiration will rapidly rise in response to the perceived threat.

Go to the ocean, however, and lie in the warm sun listening to the sound of the surf and you will, most likely, have a very different experience. Blood pressure and heart rate will lower. There will be, with most persons, an increase in Alpha/Theta and perhaps even Delta activity.

These two extremes of relaxed and alert attention comprise the continuum of outer-directed awareness.

There is also an inner-directed awareness. Dreams are a form of inner-directed awareness, which can, and often do, profoundly affect brain state. Certain types of contemplation and meditation also affect brain state. It is also possible to change brain state through a type of mental activity called fantasy. This is possible because, under the right conditions, parts of the brain cannot tell the difference between a real or an imagined event.

Let me give you an example.

In a moment, I would like you to set the book aside and for the next minute or so I would like you to remember something. I'd like you to remember a time when you felt very relaxed and comfortable. Perhaps you were floating in a warm bath, or lying out in the sun by the ocean or sitting in a big comfortable chair. Whatever the memory, I would like you to recall it in a moment. After you have called up that memory, I'd like you to experience those pleasant and relaxing sensations again as if you were actually there, in that relaxing situation. Make the scene real by adding all of your five senses. Imagine that you can see, taste, smell, hear, and feel the physical sensations just as you did originally. Let yourself luxuriate in the comfortable and relaxing feelings.

Before you begin the experience, I would like you to notice your breathing, how fast or slowly you are breathing and how tense or relaxed you feel.

Then recall the memory and enjoy the relaxed and comfortable feelings. After about a minute or so of this relaxing fantasy, note your breathing again. Notice how fast or slowly you are breathing and how tense or relaxed you feel.

Okay, now put the book aside and go through the fantasy exercise.

If you went through the above exercise, you probably noticed a change in your breathing rate and sense of relaxation. If you didn't, go back through it again and again until you feel the change. Sometimes it takes more than once to train the brain/mind to recognize a new state. Repetition is one of the keys to mastery.

What you did in this simple exercise was to alter your brain state by doing something in your mind. In addition, you changed your breathing. Remember that whenever anything changes within a system, everything in that system changes. By altering your experience in the mind (a nonphysical dimension), you have changed your breathing pattern as well as physical processes in your brain. If you had been hooked up to an EE, during this experience, we would have probably noted an increase in Alpha and/or Theta activity.

This leads us to a very important relationship within the brain/mind system, which is represented as a graph below.

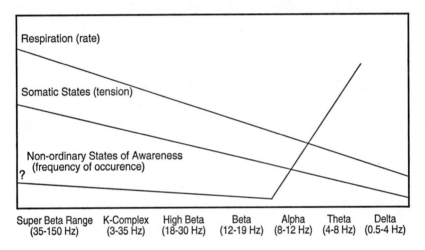

| Super Beta Range (35-150 Hz) | K-Complex (3-35 Hz) | High Beta (18-30 Hz) | Beta (12-19 Hz) | Alpha (8-12 Hz) | Theta (4-8 Hz) | Delta (0.5-4 Hz) |

Figure 8

On the far left of the graph, notice the breathing rate starts out fairly high and then slopes down towards a very low rate on the right side of the graph. Also notice that on the bottom of the graph, the brain states are laid out with High Beta on the far left and that they go down towards Delta on the right.

This graph demonstrates a fundamental relationship between the breath and brain state: as the brain state transits towards a lower rate, the breath becomes slower. Or, you could also say that as the breath gets slower and more relaxed, the brain state changes to a lower rate. They are intimately interdependent. When you change one, you change the other.

There are two other lines on the graph.

The top line is labeled "somatic states." This includes such things as muscle tension and kinesthetic sensations.

As respiration becomes slower and more relaxed, and as brain states transit from the higher rates (on the left side of the graph), to the lower rates (on the right side of the graph) there is a corresponding decrease in muscle tension. In addition, kinesthetic or physical sensations become more pleasant and comfortable. (Note: In some rare individuals, relaxation actually creates uncomfortable reactions. In such instances, I have found that these individuals usually have emotional issues around the loss of control and/or suppressed feelings. However, for the vast majority of individuals, it is true that as they become more relaxed, there is a corresponding increase in pleasure.)

This is one of the ways massage helps people to relax. By massage I don't mean those massage parlors tucked away in the back alleys of cities. I am referring to therapeutic massage, which is altogether different.

A well-trained massage therapist works the muscles, gently stretching them. Muscle tension lets go, and as this occurs other parts of the brain/mind system are affected. Breathing becomes more relaxed and slower. And there is a corresponding shift of brain state into the more relaxed areas of Alpha and Theta, sometimes even Delta.

The remaining line on the graph is labeled "non-ordinary awareness." By ordinary awareness we mean day-to-day mental realities. An example would be seeing your alarm clock sitting on your bed stand. Non-ordinary awareness is unusual. It is not the type of awareness we normally experience. An example of this is a dream in which you see the clock floating in the air above your head with the hands going backwards.

You will notice that these "non-ordinary awarenesses" on the graph take the form of a curve. This represents an observed two-fold phenomena: 1) for most people, non-ordinary states of awareness are more likely to occur in the relaxed brain states of Alpha and Theta, and 2) recent work with High Beta frequencies indicates that these states have a potential to unlock non-ordinary states of consciousness as well.

Such non-ordinary states would be very disturbing in our day-to-day activities, such as driving a car. But in a safe environment (i.e. where you do not have to pay attention to the outside world) these states are the springboards into high states of creativity and pleasure.

The "non-ordinary awareness" line goes off at both ends into a question mark. This is because we do not yet know the limits of what is possible in the non-ordinary realms of awareness. In the coming decades, I suspect that we will see a radical increase in our understanding of altered states of consciousness and their practical implications. But at present ,we are just beginning to recognize their potential.

This current state of affairs is similar to those of physics at the beginning of the nineteenth century. Researchers knew that electricity had potential as an energy source, but no one was exactly sure how to harness it.

As for harnessing the potential of your own brain states is concerned, there are four ways to proceed:

1) Change how you are breathing.
2) Change something in your mental or emotional experience.
3) Change sensory patterning (light, sound, and or kinesthetic (physical sensation) patterns).

4) Change how you are moving or holding your body.

You can also change your brain state through other ways, chemical and nutritional are examples. However, for our purposes, we will be focusing only on the above four methods. And to begin our exploration, I would like to start with the last one first — the body.

I find it especially ironic to begin our mastery of brain states through use of the body. Most people think of the brain and the body as very separate. They are not.

If you look at the diagram of the human nervous system below, you will see that it looks very much like a tree. Through the central nervous system and peripheral nerves, the brain reaches out into every part of the body. The gentle breezes that imperceptibly pass across your skin are experienced and mapped out by the brain. The brain "knows" what area of the body is sensing the breeze.

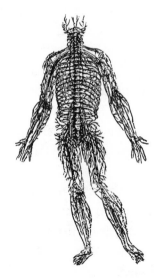

Central and Peripheral Nervous System

Figure 10

There are many ways the body affects the brain/mind system. Obviously heart and respiration are crucial. Without oxygen, the brain would die within a few minutes. If the biochemistry of digestion is not in order, the brain can be thrown out of balance due to an instability in its major food source — glucose.

Due to the system's complex interdependence on other bodily processes, we do not have the time to discuss all of the aspects. Fortunately in our attempts to change brain state through use of the body, we need only be concerned with three major areas:

1) muscle tension,

2) cerebral spinal fluid, and

3) bodily position — how you hold your body in relation to gravity.

By now the relationships between muscle tension and brain states should be clear. To summarize, we learned that as muscles "let go" of tension and relax, there is a corresponding slow down of EEG readings and a shifting into more relaxed brain states. But the relationship to cerebral spinal fluid may not be quite as clear.

The brain has open spaces inside itself called ventricles. These ventricles are, in turn, filled with a fluid called cerebral spinal fluid, which feeds and nourishes the brain.

The cerebral spinal fluid is pumped into the brain from the spinal cord, and if the cerebral spinal fluid is not flowing freely into the brain, the brain/mind system cannot operate at full performance.

The exercise you are about to do will give you an immediate change in brain state. It will circulate cerebral spinal fluid into your brain, and release tension from major muscle groups.

You will be affecting the brain/mind system by creating somatic or bodily changes.

In a moment, I will ask you to refer to the exercise below. There you will find detailed instructions for the Two Minute Stress

Buster. Go through the exercise two or three times, exactly as described.

Do not, read on until you have finished the exercise.

The Two Minute Stress Buster

Caution: Persons with low blood pressure, those prone to dizziness, or those with back problems should not do this exercise without first consulting a physician.

This is not a calisthenic exercise, though at first glance it may seem like one. Its purpose is to relax your brain state by gently stretching some of the major muscle groups, stimulating the lymph system, and circulating the cerebral spinal fluid.

After you have completed the exercise you will feel refreshed and more relaxed. It is an excellent pick-me-up.

There are two important points to the Stress Buster. You must do the movements very slowly. Never rush. Place your entire awareness or mental focus on the slow movements. Feel how one movement flows into the next, and so on. The more you focus on these slow movements with the full power of your mind, the more powerfully this exercise will alter your brain state. Through this simple exercise, you can enter a timeless space, if even only for a minute, and create a sense of relaxation and freedom.

The second important point is to make all of the movements as gentle as possible. When you get to the edge of your comfort zone, do not go past it. This is not a competition, it is a means to relax your brain state by easily stretching your muscles.

Remember three words whenever you do the Stress Buster: *slow and easy!*

Two Minute Stress Buster:

1. Stand with your feet about shoulder's length apart.
2. Imagine that you are a Raggedy Ann or Andy doll and

shake yourself from side to side. Let your arms hang limp. Shake your legs, torso, arms and head all at once. (This stimulates your lymph system.)

3. Now slowly rotate your shoulders backward in a full circle as you slowly take a full deep breath. Inhale as the shoulders go up, and slowly exhale as the shoulders go down. Pause and then reverse the direction of rotation. Slowly rotate your shoulders forward in a full circle as you again slowly take a full deep breath. Inhale as the shoulders go up, and slowly exhale as the shoulders go down.

4. Pause, and very slowly, one vertebra at a time, lower your head towards the floor. Slightly bend your knees. Allow your back to bend very slowly, one vertebra at a time, until your head is gently hanging between your knees and your arms hanging limp towards the floor. You should feel a "slight and comfortable" pull in the hamstring muscles at the back of the legs. If you do not feel a pleasant "pulling" in these muscles, bring your knees in slightly, until you feel a comfortable "pull." At no time should this stretch feel tight or uncomfortable.

5. Very slowly stretch the arms, one at a time, towards the floor. Feel the pleasant stretch in the middle of your back, as your hands and neck hang limply between your legs. Make these movements slow and be sure they are comfortable. The arms and neck should hang limp at all times.

6. Gently and ever so slightly tuck in the butt and slowly raise yourself, one vertebra at a time, reversing the direction you took down.

7. Standing with your head looking straight ahead, slowly rotate your shoulders backward. Inhale as your shoulders rise and exhale as you lower them. After you have completed the backward rotation, slowly rotate your shoul-

ders forward, again inhaling as you raise them and slowly exhaling as you lower them.
8. Notice how you are breathing and how you feel. Repeat this exercise, just as described, two more times.

If you did the exercise correctly, you will have noticed an immediate lift, a sense of relaxation and possibly pleasure.

If you did not experience any of these don't worry. It may take time. Some of us must train ourselves to even recognize that we are carrying tension. Just keep practicing the exercise, and you will eventually feel its effects.

I suggest that you do this exercise every day. I spend a lot of time at my computer or sitting while working with clients. After an hour or so my body sometimes starts to get tense from inactivity; so I've trained myself to get up and do the exercise every hour. You will be amazed at how effective it is for blowing off stress.

So far in this chapter you have had two experiences where you have changed your brain state. The first was through changing your mental and emotional experience. In that experience, you imagined what it felt like to be relaxed, and your brain/mind system adjusted itself.

In the second experience, you changed brain state by changing how you moved your body.

There is one more line on the graph that we need to explore before going into the actual exercises for mastery.

This last line is, of course, breathing.

There are innumerable ways of altering your breathing patterns. Almost all of them will change your brain state. In the chapter on breathing you will learn several different methods for changing brain state through altering your breath. But for now I would like you to try just one technique.

Level One Breathing

Caution: Persons with low blood pressure or persons who have recently suffered a stroke should consult their physician before trying this exercise. Never try this exercise while driving or in situations where alertness is required. Do not do this exercise standing up.

Level One Breathing Exercise

1. Inhale to a count of eight.

    (Each count equals about one second. Count one thousand, two thousand, three thousand, etc. to yourself.)

2. Hold (the breath in) to a count of eight.

3. Exhale to a count of eight.

4. Hold (the breath out) to a count of eight.

    Repeat the above sequence seven more times for a total of eight times.

Notice how you feel.

Do you feel more relaxed? Do you have any floating feelings? Do you seem somehow more detached from things?

These are just a few of the sensations people notice with this breathing pattern. If you did not have experiences, don't worry. It may take some practice to notice some of the more subtle changes created by alterations in breathing. Stick with it. You will soon notice all types of changes.

In this chapter, we discussed how the brain/mind system interrelates and how changing one aspect of the system alters the other aspects of the system.

In the next chapter, we will look at how you create your mental and emotional experiences; how these, in turn, affect your brain state; and how you can alter any part of your experience at will.

CHAPTER SIX

Tinker Toys of the Mind

"Use your brain for a change."
— Richard Bandleer

You are sitting up front in a darkened movie theater, and the screen looms bigger than real life. Suddenly you see a woman running down a darkened street. She looks back furtively with a terrified look on her face. She stops; she screams.

The screen flashes to a close-up of a monster bearing its fangs and growling. The camera zooms in on the beast's hideous teeth, its razor sharp fangs engulfing the entire screen. You gasp for breath....

Ah, the stuff of horror movies. The directors of celluloid realities know how we construct experience. Even if they never sat down to think it out, they know how to get us.

But what if, when the woman turned in our movie and

screamed, the camera took a long shot of the monster far off in the distance, so far in fact, that you could hardly make out what it was.

Would this new version have the same impact as the first one? Would you have gasped for breath? Probably not.

It was the sudden bigness of the picture that startled you. Take away the size, and it loses its power.

Pictures are important because that is how our brains work. The brain makes pictures of things in your mind. These pictures are records of things you have actually seen, and in some cases, imagined. Not only does the brain make pictures, it also makes sounds, feelings, sensations, tastes, and odors.

It has been said that everything you have ever experienced is recorded in your brain. Whether or not this is 100 percent accurate, it is absolutely true that everything you have experienced is coded in the form of internal representations.

In NeuroLinguistic Programming (NLP), these internal representations of the world are called "sensory modalities." Most of us have habitual ones we come back to again and again to make sense of the world.

Take for instance my first visit to New York. I had never been in a city that large before, and I had no real idea where I was when I stepped off the train. I opened a letter I had gotten from a friend with instructions to her apartment in the Italian part of town.

As I wandered from Grand Central Station to the subway I noticed the shops, the mannequins dressed in the latest fashion, and street signs. I tried to remember these things. I would need them when I retraced my tracks back to the station.

Although it was a summer afternoon twenty years ago, I can still "see" in my mind's eye the brightly colored signs and stalls of fruits and vegetables as I walked into the Italian section of the city.

I can also remember what I was feeling then — an odd mixture of curiosity, amazement, and anxiety. Until I saw the number on her building and heard her voice on the intercom, I didn't know if I was really in the right part of town or not.

How can I re-experience something that happened so long ago? How does anyone remember anything for that matter?

Well, neurologically speaking, we know that memory is organized in the brain via neurons and their vast interconnections. Just how this occurs, we don't know for sure. However, what happens in "the mind" is quite clear.

All experience is remembered in sensory fragments or bits. For instance, remember something pleasant that happened recently. Recall this pleasant experience before you go on.

Remember what you saw, now add to that what you heard, next add what you felt, —both what you felt physically and what you may have felt emotionally. By now you should have a pretty good re-creation of what you experienced. Finally, remember if there were any tastes or aromas. Add these to your remembrance.

What you noticed in the original experience is what you remember. Please note that I said "what you noticed is what you remember," and not "what happened is what you remember." There is a deeply ingrained temptation to believe that what we experience is what is actually happening.

Any good criminal attorney will tell you that this is simply not the case. In instances where two or more witnesses report on the same event, their testimony is often quite different. Each of them experienced the event. But it is how they experienced the event, and not the event itself, that they remember. To further complicate things, memories are often enhanced or changed by unconscious desires or choices.

This leads us to what, for some, may be a disturbing truth —

all of our experience is artifact.

This means that you can never directly experience reality, you can only make representations of it. Take this book, for instance. Its texture, its shape, the words on its pages, and the meaning those words convey are all experienced by you in a uniquely individual way.

My dog, Merlin, might chew on it if he were bored, but he would certainly never read it. His experience of the book is quite different than mine, as is yours.

This precariousness of perception is something most of us try to avoid. We like to pretend that we all see the same world in the same way. But such is not the case.

I recall a story I heard from several psychologists over the years about some missionaries who took a film projector and portable generator into the African bush. They set up the screen and the projector and excitedly showed scenes of the outside world to the natives. The problem was that the natives couldn't see the pictures. They hadn't seen such things and hadn't learned to see two-dimensionally. To the missionaries the screen showed a rich world of images. To the natives it was just a bunch of flickering lights. They had to be trained to see the images, which, according to the story, they finally did.

In the case of seeing, we believe that what we see is the way it is, when what we are really seeing is an internal representation of something caused by light photons stimulating nerve cells. Not only that, but the image sent to the brain is actually upside down. It is the brain that turns the image "right side up."

Further, all of our senses get "censored" as their signals are routed through the neocortex. The only exception to this is our sense of smell.

As I sit in my office typing these words into the computer, I am only aware of a few things at a time. It is difficult, for instance, for me to simultaneously think what I am going to say next; type it into the computer; watch it come up on the screen as I listen to the rain falling outside my window and the faint sound of sirens off in the distance and the music playing softly in the background; and feel the soft cool air coming in through the opened window and feel my feet against the floor.

Now if I try to do this, — be aware of as many things as I can at the same time — an interesting situation develops. I go into a receptive brain state called trance which I will explain later.

For now my point is this: I notice that the sound of the sirens has changed. There are more of them, and they seem to be all heading towards the eastern part of town. This is what I am noticing right now. If I remember this exact moment at some later time, I will "hear" the sound of the sirens in my "mind." This bit or fragment will be part of my total memory of this evening.

Now if I did not cue into or notice something I mentioned earlier, say the feel of my feet against the floor, it would not exist in my conscious memory. And if, at some later time, I recalled this exact moment, I would not feel, in my mind, my feet against the floor.

However, memory is a pliable thing. If I suggested to myself that I could feel my feet against the floor as I recall this evening, I could, in fact, create such an experience. The pliability of memory is something we will also come back to again, but for now my point has to do with how memory is constructed.

All human memories are constructed out of five bits or fragments. These are, of course, the five senses. You may have pictures in your head of an experience, or you may "hear" the sounds you heard then. You could feel the sensations and emotions you felt then, or you could, again, experience the tastes or aromas you experienced originally. And, you can experience any or all of these in any combination.

This may seem odd to you at first, but it is often not the memory itself that is compelling or powerful. But rather it is how the bits or fragments of the memory are put together that determine its strength.

For example, Todd was an attractive young man in his early twenties. He had come to see me because of depression. He had recently been "dumped" by a woman with whom he was deeply in love. No matter what he tried, Todd could not get her "out of his head."

Todd had great big technicolor pictures of this woman and his experiences with her running almost constantly through his head. They evoked all of those wonderful feelings he had felt with her, and they reminded him of his loss.

After we dealt with his belief that this was his only chance at love, an erroneous idea, but one which he believed none the less, we turned to his "pictures."

I asked Todd to change the pictures in his mind from color to black and white. I then asked him to put a frame around the pictures and then to move them off into the distance until the images were very fuzzy. I also asked him to turn the pictures upside down.

As he completed the task, I asked him how he felt about the pictures. He laughed and said they didn't bother him anymore. They seemed remote, far away.

By having Todd change how he structured his pictures, we changed his emotional reaction to a series of memories. We did not spend months in therapy going back into his childhood to uncover the roots of his obsession. We simply changed the structure of his memory so that there was nothing left to obsess about. By the way, Todd's obsession quickly faded.

The crucial question in this approach is not "why" something is happening, but rather "how" is the person creating this experience for himself. The answer will always come back, in one form or another, to these five bits or fragments called sensory modalities.

It is important to interject a caution here. In my work with Todd we did not, at first, address the underlying issue surrounding his obsession with lost love. Our first goal was to get him out of his depression so that he could cope with the immediate things in his life. But after shifting his "internal pictures," we did focus on the underlying issues which came, as is so often the case, from his childhood.

In NLP the five sensory fragments that comprise our internal representations of the world have specific names.

These are:

Visual — seeing
Auditory — hearing
Kinesthetic — physical sensation
Olfactory — smell
Gustatory — taste

The kinesthetic modality of NLP includes feeling or emotions, but in Body/Mind Re-education™[1] (B/M R) we put emotions into another category so that we can give feelings more attention.

In B/M R we call this feeling modality the "emotive." The Random House Dictionary of the English Language defines *emotion* as "an affective state of consciousness in which joy, sorrow, fear, hate, or the like, is experienced as distinguished from cognitive and volitional states of consciousness... and usu-

---

[1] Note: B/M R is a method for rapid personal transformation that re-educates the body/mind system into more resourceful states of behavior. It was developed by the author over the course of ten years, and integrates principles from NLP, Ericksonian Hypnosis, Transpersonal Psychology, Quantum Physics and Psychoacoustics.

ally accompanied by certain physiological changes such as increased heartbeat, respiration, or the like, and often overt manifestation such as crying, shaking, etc."

The root of the word *emotive* implies movement. And feelings/emotions can move with a powerful force.

To clarify the position of senses and emotions in our experience, B/M R uses a classification of "experiential modalities" rather than sensory modalities. The schema looks like this:

Experiential Modalities

Sensory Based	Sensory Related
Visual	Emotive Modality
Auditory	
Kinesthetic	
Olfactory	
Gustatory	

The Emotive Modality is placed in another column, as you can see. It is true that emotions or feelings are experienced physically and thus share a commonality with the kinesthetic modality (physical sensations). But they are quite different as well. For one thing emotions are processed by different areas of the brain than the nerve pathways of sensation. And while emotions or feelings are related to sensory perception, they cannot be reduced to the five senses. They are response patterns to sensory perception and/or beliefs about sensory perceptions.

It is here that I would wish to comment on what I consider to be a dangerous precedent in some human performance technologies such as NLP.

Some, though not all, NLP practitioners believe that they can actually bypass the emotional circuitry of the brain and disregard or subjugate emotional responses.

It is true that you can manipulate the sensory modalities in such a way as to diminish the impact of an emotional response (as I did with Todd), but that does not eliminate the response. In many cases it just goes underground only to resurface again.

This has to do with the circuitry of the brain itself. Mental experiences are created largely via the neocortex (third level) while emotions are generated from much deeper structures in the brain — the limbic/hypothalamic pathways (second level). Thus it is possible, and this often actually happens, that a person thinks they have dealt with an emotional issue when all he or she has done is "think about it."

Such persons are shocked when the issue resurfaces, sometimes with a vengeance. Thinking and emotion or feeling are not the same thing. Feelings must be dealt with in their own language which is visceral, not mental. Thoughts and feelings are neurologically different. And any psychology or human technology that diminishes or disregards the power of emotion is treading on thin ice.

In Western countries, such as the United States, the primary experiential modalities of most people are confined to the visual, auditory, kinesthetic, and emotive. It seems that the olfactory and gustatory modalities are more likely to be processed unconsciously. They seem to be, for Westerners, less prominent in the process of making sense of the world.

This is not the case in other cultures, such as the Middle East or Africa where the sense of smell and taste are very important.

This is not to say that Westerners do not have internal representations of smell and taste, just that these representations are more likely to be subjugated by the first three modalities of seeing, hearing, and feeling.

But enough *talk* about sensory modalities. Let's have you experience them for yourself. On the next few pages, you will find some sensory-based exercises. Please go through each one as outlined.

You may notice that some of these exercises seem easier for you than others. This is because you are probably more adept at one modality than another. Just go through them as best you can.

You need not do these "perfectly," whatever that is! The intent here is to give you some direct experience of your own sensory modalities.

Changing Visual Memories

Choose a visual memory of something you do not mind playing with. In other words, don't pick a memory that is important to you, or that you wish to leave intact.

1. Notice your emotional reaction to this picture in your head.
2. Notice if the picture is in color. If it is in color, change it to black and white. If it is black and white or a muted color, change it into vivid color. Notice your emotional reaction to this change.
3. Notice if the picture has a frame around it. If it does, take the frame away. If it doesn't, put a frame around the picture. Notice your emotional reaction to this new picture.
4. Notice if the picture is moving or still. If the picture is moving, slow it down until it is still. If it is still, make it moving. Notice your emotional reaction to this change.
5. Finally, notice if the picture is clear or fuzzy. If it is clear, make the picture fuzzy. If it is fuzzy, make it clear.
6. Now look at this changed picture in your mind. What is your emotional reaction to it now? Is it different than your reaction to the original picture?

Note: If you prefer this new reaction, leave the new picture in place. If you prefer your first reaction, bring the picture back to the way it was.

Changing Auditory Information

Choose an auditory memory of someone's voice you do not mind playing with. As with the previous exercise, don't pick a memory that is important to you or that you wish to leave intact. You might, for instance, recall the voice of your boss or an acquaintance.

1. Recall someone's voice. Actually "hear" it internally. Notice your emotional reaction to that voice.
2. Now speed up the sound of that person's voice so it sounds like a 33 rpm record playing at 45 or 78 rpm. Notice your emotional reaction.
3. Slow down the voice so it sounds like a 45 or 78 rpm record playing at 33 rpm. What is your emotional reaction to this voice now?
4. Bring the voice back to its normal speed and imagine some ridiculous music playing in the background. Notice your emotional reaction.
5. Bring the voice back to normal. Where does it seem to be located? Is it on the left side of your head, or the right, or is it located in the front or back of you? Wherever it is located, move the voice to the opposite side. For instance, if it is located to your left, move it to your right. Or if it is in front of you, move it to the back. If it seems to be everywhere, compress it so it comes from one point, and move the point around to find the most comfortable spot. What is your emotional reaction when you change the location of the voice?

Note: Move the voice back to where it was originally if you prefer, or leave it in this new location if you like it better.

Changing Kinesthetic Information

In this exercise we will be drawing on memories to construct internal kinesthetic experiences.

1. Imagine and feel yourself on a snow-capped mountain. Intensify the feeling. Feel the cold air on your face. Take a moment to make this experience as real as you can.
2. Next, imagine and feel yourself on a beach at summer. Intensify the feeling. Feel the warmth of the sun on your skin, and as before, take a moment to feel this sensation as much as you can.
3. Now imagine and feel yourself floating in water. Feel the temperature of the water and its sensation against your skin. For the next few moments, just enjoy the sensation of floating in water.

Emotive Information

The purpose of this exercise is to attune you to the various physiological shifts that occur with this modality of experience.

1. Recall a happy feeling. Intensify it. Make it stronger. Where do you feel this emotion most clearly in your body? Notice the physical sensations in your face as you feel this emotion.
2. Recall a sad feeling. Intensify the feeling and notice where you seem to feel this emotion. Notice the physical sensation in your face as you feel this feeling.
3. Recall an angry feeling. Intensify this feeling and notice where in your body you feel this emotion the most. Notice the physical sensations in your face as you experience this feeling.
4. Now take a deep breath and on the exhale imagine that the angry and sad feelings are leaving on the exhale. Now recall a calm feeling and take a moment to be in this calm feeling.

The olfactory and gustatory modalities will be addressed in

another chapter, but these four give us a good starting place for exploring the mind or our mental/emotional processes.

You may recall that I said earlier there is no such thing as "the mind." Rather the mind is a process that runs parallel with physical processes in the brain.

With the added dimension of experiential modalities, this becomes even clearer. Take for instance, your act of reading this book. We know that the image of its pages is actually coming into the brain upside down, and it is being flipped "right side" up in the visual centers of the brain (at the back of the head). These visual neurons actually take tiny slices of what they "see" and, it is believed, other parts of the brain put these pieces together and interpret the resulting image. By the time you actually have the experience of seeing the words on these pages, the images have been changed in hundreds, if not thousands, of ways. These permutations have taken place solely within your brain, although environmental factors can affect them.

Your experience of reading this book may be described as taking place in your mind, but this is not accurate. There is no mind for it to be in. "The mind" is more a process of noticing or being aware than a repository.

Let me once again use my "best friend" to illustrate. This afternoon I took Merlin for a walk. Spring is coming to our area, and the ornamental pear trees are laced with vibrant pink flowers. The daffodils have popped their heads out of the earth and our Holland tulips are blossoming.

As we walked down the long driveway, Merlin was off sniffing leaves and leaving his mark on the sides of trees.

For a moment, I watched him doing his dog thing rooting through the woods. I felt a warm feeling in my heart, which I often feel with him when I am feeling content. I took a deep breath and smelled the air, which was laden with perfume from all the flowers.

Then my mind "turned" to something else. I was thinking about how I should change a section of this book, and I was turning over in my mind how I would rephrase some of the sentences. For me, in that moment of introspection, the trees, Merlin, the woods and the aromas disappeared. I was "lost in thought." My attention was not on Merlin or the woods, it was on what I was thinking.

This process of shifting from one thing to another does not take place in "the mind." The mind is that very process of shifting. The mind is, quite literally, the focus of your attention.

The shocking truth is that there is no mind, only shifting attention and awareness. It is true that we have self-awareness. You are, most likely, aware that you are reading. But this does not constitute your mind. It is your attention to the act of reading that is creating your mental experience of reading. Quickly turn your attention now to something else. Put the book down for a moment and look at something else around you in the environment. Take a moment to experience this thing. Do this now.

As you are now reading again, that thing you looked at a moment ago is probably still there. It just isn't in your mind anymore, unless you remember it. This is because you have shifted your attention to notice something else.

But, just because you haven't noticed something, obviously doesn't mean that it's not there. And it may even be affecting you without your knowing it.

Our mental and emotional experience can be divided into roughly two areas — conscious awareness and unconscious awareness.

Due to the way our brains are "wired," we can only be conscious of a few things at a time. But we are actually aware of much more than we can ever be conscious of. There are ways to tap into and utilize this vast unconscious awareness, which we will explore later.

For now my main concern is that we understand the true nature of "the mind" as a shifting of attention or awareness.

I also hope by now that it is clear to you that our awareness of the world is an artifact, that we do not experience anything directly. Rather, we make internal representations of the world. These representations will always take the form of what we see, hear, feel, taste, and smell. And, we may have emotional or feeling responses to our perceptions, real or imagined.

The ability to alter our internal sensory-based experiences or internal representations is a powerful tool. And it is one you will learn to use in the course of these pages.

I called this chapter "Tinker Toys of the Mind" because the elements that create our mental and emotional experience (call it "the mind" if you wish) are very much like Tinker Toys. Although our minds are vast and complicated processes, they are built upon tiny little pieces.

Some of these pieces are the experiential modalities with which we just dealt. Another piece is something called anchoring.

Anchoring is a term that refers to the creation of specific mental and emotional states.

Before NLP, it was called "paired associative learning." I think anchoring is a much more descriptive term. It probably seems that way to me because my father was in the Navy.

I remember once when my dad took me out on the water in a fishing trawler. The captain of the old, rusty hulk had known my dad for years.

As we neared shore we "dropped anchor," and I helped toss a big rusty piece of metal tied to a long rope into the water. The rope hissed as it uncoiled itself following the anchor into the watery depths. Finally the rope stopped running, and all was silent save the sound of waves against the hull and the cawing of sea birds.

I watched as the incoming tide tried to pull the boat ashore, but each time the rope would pull taut, the anchor dug into the sea bed somewhere below us and held us in position.

Each of us has hundreds of such anchors that we use every day, except these anchors are not tied to the hull of a boat. They are tied to our emotions and our motivations.

Do you wash your face or take a shower in the morning when you get up? If so, this is an anchor. Morning, for you, automatically means washing your face or showering. You don't really think about it now, do you? You just sort of wander into the bathroom on semi-automatic.

By going through these actions, year after year, you have built them into a habit or reflex, and this reflex is connected to the act of the sun rising.

If you have to think about it, it is not an anchor. Anchors are automatic and do not require contemplation or figuring out. They are a function of the brain's ability to associate things together.

This association does not need to be, and often is not, logical. The brain is not scanning for logic here. It is simply associating one event with another. These perceived events are, of course, always experienced in the form of sensory modalities.

Take advertising for instance.

Advertising is the art and science of anchoring other people so that they will buy products, even if they don't need them. In no other human endeavor is the truth more clearly seen that anchoring need not be logical.

I recently saw a television ad for popcorn. A very sexy woman was sprawled across a sofa as she devoured a bag of popped corn. I am told that the ad has been very successful.

So how did it get our attention? Sex.

The brain is always scanning the environment for different

types of stimulation. If you are hungry, your brain looks for food, even if you aren't aware of it. Your brain may also be scanning for status and power. In such cases, scenes of social status will catch your attention. Look at the ads for luxury items, and you will see this quite clearly.

And of course, one of the brain's main forms of stimulation is sexual. In a man or woman of reproductive age, the brain is often scanning for sex. It is "wired in." Now, in some people this sexual desire may be masked over or even subdued by other interests, but as a whole, the American culture is obsessed with sex. And Madison Avenue knows this.

So what does popcorn have to do with sex? Nothing. And that is my point. By showing a picture of someone sexy doing sexy things, and then flashing back and forth to her eating popcorn, the brain associates this kind of popcorn with sex. And voila, if you are one of those millions scanning for sex, the ad will catch your attention, even if not consciously. You have, my friend, been anchored. And the next time you are at the store buying popcorn or perhaps just seeing popcorn on the shelf, the odds are that you will buy that brand to which you were anchored.

Anchors often take the form of emotions. Have you ever had the experience of seeing someone you didn't like and having an emotional reaction at just the sight of them? You didn't need even to interact with them, to have that reaction.

The sight of them or the mentioning of their name can become an anchor to unpleasant experiences in the past. These uncomfortable reactions have become associated with their face, their name, and sometimes with their voice. And conversely, people with whom we have had positive interactions become pleasurable anchors. Seeing them, hearing their voices, or hearing their names can produce immediate and pleasurable responses.

We are continually being anchored by experiences in our

lives. And given their power to affect us, wouldn't it be a good idea to know how to anchor yourself? Like the experiential modalities mentioned earlier, this "Tinker Toy" of the mind is built on very simple pieces. After you have mastered putting together and taking apart these pieces, you will have a tremendous power at your disposal — the ability to change your motivations and experience at will.

Anchors Away

1. Sit comfortably and close your eyes.
2. Recall a pleasant experience, something that gives you pleasure to think about.
3. Now extract from that experience the feeling of pleasure. Your focus, in other words, is not on the experience, but on the feeling of pleasure itself.
4. Now make this feeling of pleasure stronger. Make it as strong as you can.
5. As you recreate this strong and pleasant feeling, let your body get into a position where the feeling is the strongest. For instance, if you felt proud, you might sit or stand upright. If you were feeling sad, you might slump over. Whatever the feeling you have chosen to recreate, let your body be in the position that feels natural to you for this feeling. As you feel the feeling and hold your body in this natural position, touch your thumb and first finger together, or reach down and touch your thigh. Sense this gesture at the same time you feel the intensified pleasant feeling. Hold the touch, your body position, and the feeling together for a few moments.
6. Release the touch and the feeling. Bring yourself back to neutral, that is, with no particular feeling.

7. Now, without changing your feeling, touch yourself in the exact same way, and at the exact same location, as you move your body into the position you took in #5.

8. Notice that as you hold this touch and this position, the feeling tends to come back.

9. Go through this exercise again and again until you feel these two anchors (your touch and body position) stimulating that pleasant feeling. Sometimes the anchors take hold after the first try. Sometimes several are required.

Do not be impatient with yourself if you do not get it the first time. Remember that mastery comes from repetition.

Sliding Anchors

1. First practice this move: with one of your hands resting on your thigh, move it down near the knee. Now slowly move the hand by dragging it up your thigh towards your waist. This movement is called a "sliding anchor," and we will use it to intensify a feeling.

2. Place your hand on your thigh down near the knee.

3. Recall a pleasant feeling, perhaps the one you created in the earlier exercise.

4. Imagine that you can intensify that feeling by sliding your hand up your thigh. Slide your hand slowly up the thigh as you intensify the feeling. When your hand gets up near your waist, the feeling should be at its maximum intensity.

5. Slowly slide your hand back down the thigh towards the knee and notice that the feeling gets less and less intense.

6. Slide your hand up and down your thigh several times until you are clear that this movement upward intensifies the feeling, and the movement downward decreases the feeling.

7. After you have done this successfully several times go on

to another feeling. Choose something such as inner peace, excitement, amusement, or one of your own.

Through these two exercises you changed your emotional state with a gesture, body position, and/or touch. There is no logical connection between feeling pleasure and what you did to create it. However, your brain linked the two together (pleasure and touch/body position) because they occurred simultaneously.

The neurological strategy is much like the sexy popcorn ad I mentioned earlier.

With a little practice, you could build in a response so that whenever you touch yourself in this way or hold this body position, you will feel the same state of pleasure.

In fact, that is what I suggest you do for the next few days. There is something very empowering in recognizing that you can change your experience at will.

Although the anchors we were using were kinesthetic, anchors can come in any sensory or experiential modality. Some people, for instance, react with fear when they are in the presence of someone who is angry. For them, anger is an anchor for fear. Anchors can also take some interesting turns.

I remember an odd experience I had in a restaurant several years ago. It was a diner with old salt and pepper shakers, the kind where the tops are rounded metal. As I sat at the table looking at the light reflecting off the sides of the salt shaker, I had the distinct memory of my grandmother's apartment.

After a few moments of very clear memories and childhood feelings, I realized what had happened. The top of the salt shaker was the same shape as the end of her old vacuum cleaner, and as a child I often spent time looking at the light reflecting off the rounded metal cap of her vacuum.

Even after all those years, light reflecting off rounded metal fired off an anchor from childhood.

Anchors can also be auditory. The sound of a person's voice or a song from one's past can fire off powerful feelings and memories, and, of course, aromas and tastes have the same power.

It is a little unconventional to look at our past in this way, but if you think of your personal history as a series of anchors it becomes more understandable in terms of how the brain experiences things.

If, for instance, your experience with your mother was nurturing, supportive, and trusting, your brain will have anchored these experiences and feelings with the images and ideas of woman and mother.

However, if your experience with Mom was one of manipulation, uncaring, and distrust, your brain will have anchored these feelings and experiences. The result would be difficulty in feeling trust or caring in relationship to women.

Again, it isn't logic we are dealing with here; it's the power of anchors [association]. A general rule of thumb is that the more intense the experience, the more powerful the anchor that was associated with it.

This is one of the reasons why violent events in our past may still affect us years later. And by violent I don't necessarily mean just physical violence. Mental and emotional violence can anchor us into distressing states just as well. But with a knowledge of anchoring and experiential modalities, you can change that.

As we go through the next chapters, you will discover how you can create powerful ways to motivate yourself. But the techniques we will be developing require that you fully understand how to change your inner experiences and how to anchor yourself.

Take some time out this week and go back over the exercises in this chapter until you can do them instantly and successfully.

CHAPTER SEVEN

Breathing Patterns
for Changing Brain States

"Excitement without breath is anxiety."

— *Fritz Perls*

The billions of cells that make up your body require regular doses of a clear and odorless gas. It is produced, for the most part, by plants, from the great trees of the Tropical rain forests to the algae floating on the surface of the earth's oceans. This gas is, of course, oxygen.

As every high school biology student knows, plants, such as trees, "breathe in" carbon dioxide and "breathe out" oxygen. It is this symbiotic relationship between plant life and animal life that sustains our very existence.

Man can live for long stretches of time without food and even for several days, without water, but we cannot live without oxygen for longer than a few minutes.

Oxygen is the stuff of which our life is made, and without it, the galaxies of neurons within our brains will die.

This is true for all reptiles and mammals. And it is from these forms of life that we have inherited both the abilities and the limitations of respiration.

Our breathing is controlled automatically from the deepest structures of the brain. We don't think about it. We do not even notice it, unless we are trying to catch our breath from exertion, or the system gets damaged by illness.

You have no sensation or awareness, for instance, that the respiratory center in your brain is now monitoring the CO_2 gases in your blood stream. When the CO_2 levels reach a certain point, you will automatically take a breath.

We share this automatic nature of breathing with other forms of animal life, from lizards and frogs on up to baboons.

In addition to being able to live without paying much attention to our breathing, we also have an innate ability to change our breathing patterns, consciously and at will.

Millennia ago, sages and yogis discovered that they could radically affect their states of consciousness by altering their breathing. In India an entire science of breathing called *pranayama* developed over the course of several centuries. Researchers have been documenting and verifying the effects of specific pranayama techniques, and many of them are very helpful to modern man.

According to this Indian system, the air is charged with a form of life force called *prana*. Prana is breathed in along with oxygen, but it is not oxygen. It is subtler. Indeed, modern science has yet to verify the existence of prana, and if the ancient rishis are correct, its substance is so subtle it will be some time before our instruments are sensitive enough to detect its presence.

The ancient Chinese Taoists called this substance *chi* or vital force.

Both prana and chi are believed to be strongest in natural settings such as forests, lakes, and oceans. This may account for part of the reason why natural environments are experienced by many as enlivening. This may also be part of the reason why some people experience cities with their wanton destruction of plants and their covering of the earth with concrete as depleting.

The neural pathways in the brain that allow us to consciously change our breathing patterns are quite extensive, and fortunately the knowledge of where and how they work is not needed to change brain states.

Breathing patterns are intimately entwined with our emotional states. Anger, for instance, can produce a volatile and deep form of breathing, while in depression, people usually take in shallow breaths. Every emotion has its corresponding breathing pattern unique to that individual. And it is physiologically difficult to experience a given emotional state while breathing the pattern of another emotion. For instance, try to be depressed and breathe the deep and rapid breathing pattern characteristic of anger. You will find that it cannot be done.

In addition to sustaining life, breathing patterns can open the doors to altered states of awareness. Such states can then be very useful for a number of practical reasons, which you will soon discover.

In the following breathing protocols, you will learn how to change your brain state in several ways. These techniques will then be used throughout the rest of the book to shift your state in preparation for different tasks, such as decreasing anxiety or increasing creativity.

I suggest that you go through each of these breathing protocols several times so that you can clearly experience their effects. It is important that you master these techniques before you go on to the next chapters.

Cautions: Persons with low blood pressure or persons who have recently suffered a stroke should consult their physician before trying any of these exercises. Never try these exercises while driving or in situations where alertness is required. Do not do these exercises standing up.

Level One Breathing

This form of breathing was described in Chapter 5, and takes you into an open and receptive brain state.

1. Inhale to a count of eight. (Each count equals about one second. Count one thousand, two thousand, three thousand, etc.,)
2. Hold (the in breath) to a count of eight.
3. Exhale to a count of eight.
4. Hold (the out breath) to a count of eight.

Repeat the sequence seven more times for a total of eight times.

Get a feel for your body; notice how relaxed it is. Notice your orientation in space. Does your body seem to be "floaty?"

Level Two Breathing

This form of breathing takes you into a deeper and more receptive state than Level One Breathing.

1. Inhale to a count of twelve.

(Each count equals about one second. Count one thousand, two thousand, three thousand, etc.)

2. Hold (the in breath) to a count of twelve.
3. Exhale to a count of twelve.
4. Hold (the out breath) to a count of twelve.

Repeat the sequence eleven more times for a total of twelve.

Note: Many people are unable to complete this protocol, since it profoundly alters awareness. Just do as much of the sequence as is comfortable. With more practice, you will be able to do more.

Get a feel for your body. How much more relaxed are you now than with Level One Breathing? What is your body's orientation in space? Does it feel "floaty?" If so, are the "floaty" feelings stronger than with Level One Breathing?

Noise Removal Breathing

This protocol was developed by Win Wenger, E.Ed., one of the nation's foremost experts on genius and intelligence.

It is based on a concept drawn from Information Theory which says that all forms of communication, whether verbal or non-verbal, follow similar basic laws. One of the fundamental concepts developed from observations about communication is termed "noise." Anything which disrupts or alters clarity of communication is called "noise."

If, for instance, you were listening to someone speak and an airplane flew nearby, the words (information) would be lost in the "noise" of the airplane. And if you were making a phone call, and the connection were bad, the static would be called "noise." If it is too strong, you could not understand the person on the other end.

"Noise" is not only external. It can also be internal. Internal "noise" is caused by such things as wandering thoughts, mental agitation, and tension. It can also be caused by chemical contaminants in the body that affect neurological functioning.

Have you ever been really fatigued and tried to follow a conversation? Have you ever found it hard to concentrate? Or have you ever found it difficult to focus on what you were doing because you were agitated or tense? This is "noise."

Applying the concepts of Information Theory to communication within the brain itself, we can see how internal "noise" can affect mental clarity.

This protocol can be used to dramatically decrease internal "noise" thereby improving mental function.

Later you will discover how to use this breathing technique in connection with other protocols to increase both creativity and performance.

The Technique
1. Sit comfortably and close your eyes.
2. Imagine and feel that your body is a hollow tube and that as you inhale, the breath is drawn up through your feet and into your legs; up into your pelvis and stomach; up into your chest and back; and up into your shoulders, neck, and head.
3. Imagine and feel your breath "swishing" through this hollow tube of your body and carrying away any tension, stress, or uncomfortable feelings.
4. When you get to the top of the inhale, just relax and exhale through normal means. Let each exhale be more relaxed than the one before it.
5. Let your breathing be long, slow and comfortable. Breathe in this way for two to five minutes — longer if you wish.

How do you feel? Is your body relaxed? What is your body's spatial orientation? Do you feel "floaty?" Floaty, relaxed feelings are a signature of lowered brain wave activity, and a goal of these techniques.

There is one other breathing technique I would like you to experience. It is a yogic breathing pattern, called Calm Breathing and is a great method for lowering brain wave activity.

Calm Breathing Protocol
1. Sit comfortably or lie down.
2. Breathe in long, slow comfortable inhales.

3. Make each exhale about the same length as the inhale.
4. Make each exhale more relaxed than the one before it.

Breathe in this way for two to five minutes to get the feel of how this method relaxes you. We will come back to it again later in this book.

As I mentioned earlier, you should practice the above exercises several times. Get a clear sense of how they affect you. Which of them takes you into the deepest state of relaxation? Which of them allows you to clearly process mental thoughts while being relaxed?

If you practice the previous four breathing protocols, you will have all you need to alter your brain state through how you breathe. As we go into the next several chapters, this knowledge will be important.

CHAPTER EIGHT

Stress Management

*"Learn to get in touch with the silence within yourself
and know that everything in this life has a purpose."*
– Elisabeth Kubler-Ross

J ay Segal, Ph.D., one of the foremost experts on stress in
America, has made the cryptic observation that there is no
such thing as stress. What does he mean by this?

He is not referring to the biochemical and biological effects of
stress. These have been extensively documented and are now
universally accepted by science. What he is referring to is the
psychological response to stressors.

If you take three people, for example, and put them in the
same "stressful" situation, say a relationship problem, chances
are that the three people will react in very unique and different
ways. One might get hostile, the other might get depressed, while
the third might attempt to work out a solution.

In other words, it is not the event that creates stress in our lives. It is our response to the events in our lives that creates our stress.

This may be hard to grasp since so many of us have been led to believe that things "happen" to us. In this scenario, it is easy to feel like victims, as if events are beyond our control. And while it may be true that some events are beyond our control, our reactions to those events are definitely within our control — that is if we choose to take control of our reactions.

You may recall that I have said that experience is artifact. We do not experience life directly. We merely make mental and emotional representations of our experience. This process is even further removed from "reality" because our representations are not of what actually happens, but rather they are representations of our experiences of what happens, a very different situation indeed.

Suppose, for instance, you were to come home on a Friday, after a long week of work to find that your bank had made a blatant error in your account, and according to the bank you owed a large sum of money. This would, for most people, be a stressful situation.

But your experience of it would be totally your creation. Some people might "stew" and get angrier and angrier, letting it spoil their entire weekend and possibly ruin the weekend of those around them. Some might feel overwhelmed and depressed as if this were further evidence that the universe was out "to get them." Still others might realize that there was nothing they could do about it until Monday, and so they would turn their attentions to other things.

These are very different styles of dealing with the same event. It is not the event itself that creates our stress, but again, our reaction or ways of dealing with it.

For our purposes, we are going to define stress very simplistically. Stress is tension.

Does this mean that when I play tennis and my arm tenses, ready to hit the ball, that I am under stress? In a sense I am, but this is enjoyable stress.

However, if I were to keep tensing my arm for hours and days at a time without relief, this form of enjoyable stress would quickly turn into displeasure.

Mental stress is a little harder to get hold of since you can't see it, and much of the time people don't know when they are feeling it. Our systems are extremely adaptive and flexible. But just because we do not consciously know we are under stress, doesn't mean it is not affecting us.

Remembering that the brain and mind are one interconnected system, I'd like you to try this little experiment.

Get a sense of the tension in your face and forehead. The fine muscles in your forehead are called your frontalis muscles, and they are a great barometer of your state of tension or relaxation. In fact, when doing electroencephalogram (EEG) measurements, the frontalis is almost always "hooked up" since it is such a clear indicator of tension.

Notice how tight or relaxed this area feels to you now.

Next, I'd like you to solve a difficult math problem. For some of you it may be as simple as multiplying three or four large numbers together in your head. You mathematicians may need to solve an entire group of equations. Whatever causes you to really have to concentrate is what is needed here.

Now notice the tension level in your forehead as you try to solve this problem. Are you aware of more tension in your forehead area?

If you didn't notice tension in this area, the math problem was not hard enough. Make the problem harder and go through the exercise again and again until you clearly feel an increase in tension in the frontalis muscles.

This increase in tension was caused simply by the act of concentrating. Have you ever had to concentrate on something for long periods of time and when you finished you discovered you were weary or tired?

The process of concentration creates muscle tension. Many people who suffer from tension headaches are the victims of their own stress pattern. While medications can often stop a tension headache, similar relief can often be accomplished by taking the time to shift Brain State.

We all have our own "brain state profile" to which we habitually return. Some people are more active and alert, while others are more relaxed and "laid back." These styles of brain function have direct ramifications on our mental and physical health.

Chronic tension, for example, caused by a hyper-alertness to the environment or a hostile attitude, can lead to gastrointestinal problems such as ulcers. Does this mean that all people with ulcers are hostile? Definitely not, but emotional states such as chronic hostility can increase the amount of digestive acids in the stomach.

In the course of each day, we are subjected to hundreds of situations that can potentially create stress responses in us. Whether or not they do this depends on how we react to them.

Most of our reactions to stress are automatic. We do not think about them. They just happen, seemingly beyond our control.

The boss comes in and tells you that you have to work late tonight. Your two-year-old has wandered off in the grocery store and turns over a display of glass jars. Your mechanic calls and says that the repairs on your car will cost three times what you and he thought they would. These situations and others like them create stress, or tension.

Each of us has a unique way of responding to stress induced tension. Some of us get headaches. Some of us get nervous. Some of us get angry and some of us get depressed. The list goes on and on.

Our reactions to stressors are individual, but they all have one thing in common. They create varying degrees of muscle tension. For our purposes, I am using a very narrow definition of stress. Stress is a body/mind response to an event or situation that generates tension whether consciously detected or not.

I would like to add here that there are a whole group of stressors of which we rarely become conscious. These include sub-conscious programmings, pollutants, and chemical and environmental irritants. They often affect us without our conscious awareness.

Part of the problem with stressors is that we are often not aware that we have reacted to them. For some of us, it is only after a few hours of them that we suddenly have a "splitting headache." In most cases, if we had paid attention to our level of tension beforehand, we could have avoided the headache or other reactions altogether.

But to do this, we must be aware when we are tensing up. The best way to become aware of tension is to become aware of what it feels like to be relaxed. It sounds odd that we would have to train ourselves to relax, in order to recognize when we are tense, but that is exactly the case.

In the exercise below, you will be asked to tense different areas of your body and then to suddenly relax them. By doing this exercise over the course of several days, you will begin to be able to tell the difference between being tense and relaxed. You will then be able to spot "little" tensions, and by the time you reach this point in your growing awareness of bodily tension, you will be able to recognize when you are under stress.

Bodily Tension Awareness Exercise

1. Lie down and get comfortable.
2. Tense your feet and calves. Hold for a count of five. Release the tension.
3. Tense your thighs. Hold for a count of five. Release the tension.
4. Tense your buttocks. Hold for a count of five. Release the tension.
5. Tense your stomach. Hold for a count of five. Release the tension.
6. Tense your chest and shoulders. Hold for a count of five. Release the tension.
7. Tense your arms and hands. Hold for a count of five. Release the tension.
8. Tense your neck. Hold for a count of five. Release the tension.
9. Tense your face. Hold for a count of five. Release the tension.
10. Now tense your entire body, from head to toe. Hold for a slow count of five. Release the tension.
11. Repeat #10 two more times.
12. Pause for a moment, and move your awareness into your body. How do you feel? (Take thirty seconds to a minute).

Step Two - Subtle Tension

Proceed into this part of the exercise immediately upon finishing step #12. The idea is to begin to become increasingly aware of subtle or light tension.

13. Gently tense the area around your eyes. The tension should be light, just enough for you to notice. Hold for a count of two. Release the tension.

14. Gently tense your ears. Hold for a count of two. Release the tension.
15. Gently tense the area around your nose. Hold for a count of two. Release the tension.
16. Gently tense your forehead. Hold for a count of two. Release the tension.
17. Gently tense the corners of your mouth. Hold for a count of two. Release the tension.
18. Gently tense your jaw. Hold for a count of two. Release the tension.
19. Gently tense your tongue. Hold for a count of two. Release the tension.

After you have completed #19, do some Noise Removal Breathing (Chapter 7) for a couple of minutes. Let any residue of tension drift away on each exhale.

Repeat this exercise at least once a day for the next week. It will attune you to an awareness of the difference between tension and relaxation. Through this simple exercise, you will soon be able to spot subtler and less obvious forms of stress-induced tension. And this awareness will serve you in the management of your stress.

Now that you are learning to recognize bodily tension, you are ready to begin managing your stress by shifting brain states.

This would be a good time to do the Two-Minute Stress Buster from Chapter 5.

Notice how much more relaxed you feel.

Part of the management of stress through brain states is being aware when you are under stress. While many of the stress factors in your life may elude you, it is quite possible to monitor your own level of muscle tension. Remember our simple definition of stress — stress equals tension.

If you become aware of the subtle tensions in your body, you can deal with them before you get into a full-blown stress reaction.

The protocols in this chapter will allow you to de-stress yourself, and they will accomplish this by shifting your brain state through the aid of your breathing and your mental processes.

Let's go through some of them and experience for yourself what they do. Then we will put them together for an effective Stress Management Program.

Relief Breathing

This is another of Dr. Win Wenger's protocols, and I have used it and taught it to hundreds of people with great success.

It allows you to quickly "let go" of troublesome feelings and hassles by activating the automatic response systems of your body and mind.

1. Sit or stand comfortably and pretend that a situation or hassle that is "bugging" you is in the form of a stuffy suit of armor.
2. Imagine yourself completely enclosed in this suit of armor. It limits your movements, your breathing and your vision. You are completely hemmed in by this imaginary suit of armor. Feel the armor compressing and weighing in on you. Do this until it seems quite real to you.
3. Now imagine taking off the armor completely. As you take off that oppressive armor take your first breath in freedom. Feel what it would feel like to take your first breath after actually taking off an oppressive suit of armor.
4. For the next two minutes or so, breathe deeply, as if each breath was your very first breath after having taken off that suit of armor.

This pattern of breathing predisposes your brain/mind system to relieve itself of whatever has been bothering it.

It is a great exercise to do when you get home from a "hard day" at work or any time you feel burdened by pressures or hassles. Some people have even used it successfully in coping with illnesses.

The process takes only about four or five minutes, and you can do this type of "imagery breath work" under almost any situation where you have a little private time.

Unstress Yourself

This protocol takes about fifteen to twenty minutes and is a great way to unwind from a "long day." It can easily follow the Relief Breathing exercise above.

It uses a combination of the breath and sensory modalities to produce a very pleasing and relaxed state of mind and body.

If you have access to a tape player, play the Creative Imagining tape (offered in Appendix B) or some other kind of music that you find relaxing.

1. Do the Two-Minute Stress Buster.
2. Sit comfortably, and for the next three minutes or so, use the Noise Removal Protocol (Chapter 7).
3. As you "settle in" and feel more relaxed, imagine yourself at a relaxing vacation spot. This may be by the ocean or in the mountains or in some other location. It may actually exist, or it may totally or partially be a creation of your imagination. What matters most is that this spot be so pleasing and relaxing that just the thought of it brings you a sense of calm and comfort.
4. After you have imagined yourself at this location, begin to make it more real. See it, hear the sounds, and feel the pleasing physical sensations and comforting emotions you would feel if you were actually there. The more real

you make it, the more powerful it will be.

5. Begin to sense your imaginary body moving through this fantasy world. Enjoy the experience. If something appears or happens in your fantasy that you don't like, remember that you are in control and change it.

6. Imagine that you have found a beautiful and ideal spot to rest. Perhaps it looks over a large body of water or something else that is pleasant to you.

7. Imagine that this spot is surrounded by beautiful flowers whose aroma you find particularly pleasing. Choose an aroma that you actually enjoy, like the smell of vanilla, or freshly baked bread, or the aroma of something else special to you. Imagine that these fantasy flowers emanate this aroma. And begin to breathe a slow and calm breathing pattern (with your "real" body).

Imagine and feel that as you breathe deeply, you can actually smell this beautiful aroma. And that as you continue breathing in this way, you reward each inhale with the delicious aroma you have chosen. Imagine and feel that every cell of your body is drinking in this aroma. Sense the sweet smell moving down and throughout your body with each breath.

8. For the next five to ten minutes, continue to breathe this long, slow, and calm breathing pattern, drawing in the sweet aromas with each breath.

9. When the time is up, let your breath return to normal, and notice how you feel. Take a few moments to be with yourself before moving back into activity.

By changing your breathing patterns and by focusing on pleasing and relaxing internal images, sounds, feelings, and smells, you can produce very relaxed states of awareness. With the above exercises, you have radically changed your own "brain state." By incorporating these into your daily life, you will be able to greatly reduce stress-induced tension and thereby increase your sense of well being as well as performance.

But no discussion of stress management would be complete without bringing our attention to something called meditation.

The word meditation has become very common in our vocabulary, but there is a lot of confusion about what meditation really is.

Some people have images of yogis sitting cross-legged in caves, while others think of it as some kind of cult activity. Actually, meditation is very simple. It is a kind of focused attention. And although there are literally hundreds, if not thousands, of meditation forms, they all share this one thing in common: focus. Some of the forms focus on the breath and some on imaginary sounds; some forms use a visual focus such as looking at a candle or a picture and some focus on body movements.

As you turn attention to a point of focus, and keep awareness there, some very interesting things happen. Bodily tension decreases, heart rate and respiration slow down, and you feel more and more relaxed.

This is why meditation is so effective as a stress management tool. Meditation also is gaining a professional acceptance in the medical community. The oldest, and considered by many to be the best stress management program in the United States is at the University of Massachusetts Medical Center in Worcester. The program, founded in 1979, uses a Buddhist-style of meditation called "mindfulness," in which awareness is focused on itself. While the technique comes from the Buddhist tradition, it is hardly a religious activity. It simply takes advantage of the body/mind's interconnectedness. At the Stress Reduction and

Relaxation Program at Worcester, housewives and businessmen, construction workers and teachers all learn and benefit from this simple meditation form.

Studies conducted at the center for the last several years have documented the amazing benefits of meditation. Psoriasis (a painful ailment of the skin) improves faster in those persons who meditate and undergo psychotherapy than in control groups who only go through psychotherapy.

An extensive four-year study of meditators showed that symptoms associated with anxiety, depression, irritability, and chronic pain were greatly reduced in those patients who meditated.

According to Dr. Steven Locke, a professor of psychiatry at Harvard Medical School, "Every community hospital and academic center ought to have a program like this."

In other words, everyone would benefit from regular meditation. If the word meditation still puts you off, try the phrase "regular systemic stabilization," for that is what meditation does. By quietly focusing your attention inward, you lower your heart rate and decrease respiration and bodily tension thereby allowing the body/mind to stabilize itself and to recover from the damaging effects of stress-induced tension.

One of the most effective meditative techniques for stress management is something called Transcendental Meditation or TM. TM's effects on the body/mind have been studied more extensively than any other meditation form, and its stress management abilities are unquestionable. I have practiced the technique for over 18 years and found it to be extremely beneficial. You can find TM centers throughout the world, and most major cities have centers whose phone numbers are listed in the phone book.

TM requires one-on-one instruction. And some people find

the process of getting "initiated" cumbersome. However, for its general accessibility, the on-going support that is available from the TM organization, and for its remarkable effectiveness, TM is probably one of the best meditation forms available for the management of stress.

There is another meditation technique which is easily learned and does not require one-on-one instruction.

Unlike some meditation forms, it does not involve trying to "still the mind." Many people find it difficult to avoid thinking in meditation. I have found that many people say they cannot meditate because it was too difficult.

This technique does not involve trying to "still the mind" at all. It does not engage thoughts, and it is so easy and so effective, I have taught it to hundreds of people over the years.

The technique comes from an ancient body of knowledge known as Taoist Yoga. Its roots go back to ancient China, where Chinese mystics and sages, called Taoists, fathomed the body/mind connection. Their abilities to alter consciousness and to affect bodily processes are legend.

The technique is called "Heaven's Gate Meditation." The location of "Heaven's Gate," according to the Taoist masters, is about one inch behind the bridge of the nose. According to this system, the gate is about one inch square and is where the cosmic forces of the heavens meet the terrestrial forces of earth within the human body.

The technique involves focusing awareness on this spot, one inch behind the bridge of the nose. What is interesting from a brain physiology point of view is that this spot is close to the hypothalamus and pituitary gland. The pituitary is sometimes referred to as the master gland since it regulates the other endocrine glands of the body.

Once in a seminar, I instructed everyone in how to use this

technique. As part of the training, we met again a month later. A woman, who had had a history of painful menstrual cramps and complications, had not had a period in almost a year. Within a couple of weeks of doing the meditation, she suddenly got her period. The meditation had re-balanced her endocrine system. And several months later, her periods continued to be regular and comfortable.

The technique produces deep states of rest, and I have often used it when traveling across time zones. Sometimes, when traveling, it is almost impossible for me to get to sleep since my biological clock is set for another time zone.

By practicing the meditation form lying down, I have been able to rest throughout the night and get up in the morning refreshed and ready to go.

One of the more humorous moments in teaching this technique occurred when my wife, Pam, and I went to Hong Kong to conduct corporate trainings in accelerated productivity. As part of the seminar for Human Development Trainers, we instructed them in the use of this ancient Taoist practice. While some of the trainers were European and American, most of them were Chinese. There was something odd about an American teaching Chinese persons something from their own cultural inheritance! Unfortunately, in their rush to Westernize, many people from other cultures have abandoned their cultural treasures. The Heaven's Gate Meditation is one such treasure.

Heaven's Gate Meditation

1. Sit comfortably with your spine erect, and your legs stretched out in front of you. (If you are using this technique in lieu of sleep, you can lie down, but you will want to have pillows by your sides to prop up your arms so you can do the "mudras.") However, generally speaking, it is

better to sit up when doing this technique.

2. Open your left palm, and place the thumb of your right hand gently into the center of your left palm (the "x" spot in the diagram below), while placing your right index finger gently on the back of the left hand directly opposite your thumb that is resting in the center of the left palm (see diagram). This gesture or "mudra" closes the "energy circuit" of your body. During the meditation, you will be circulating energy, and this mudra will help you to keep the energy inside. Rest both hands held in this position on your lap or chest, so that it takes no energy to hold up your hands.

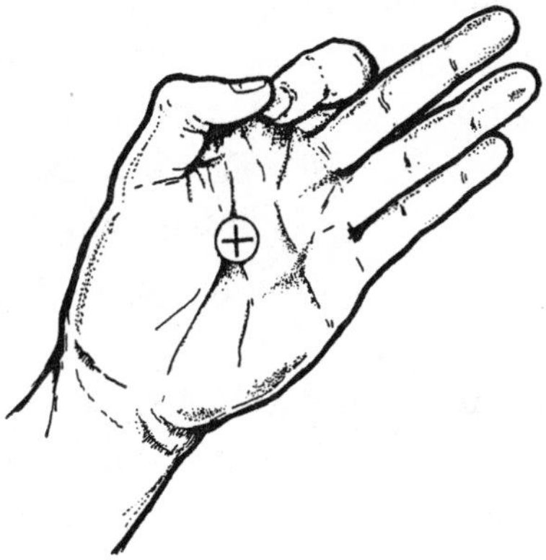

Figure 11

3. Cross your left foot over your right foot, and let it rest there. If you are left handed, you may want to try resting your right foot over your left foot.

4. Rest your tongue against the roof of your mouth or against the back of your teeth. This closes the "internal circuit" or "microcosmic orbit." The microcosmic orbit is the route through which life force or "chi" rises up the spine and circulates through the brain and moves down the front of the body back down to the perineum. When it moves

down the front of the body it is called the "Governing Meridian" due to its influence on a large number of organs. The tongue acts as a switch. When the tongue is not touching the roof of the mouth the circuit is "open" and there is no flow of chi through the "orbit." However, when the tongue is at the roof of the mouth the circuit is "closed" and chi can freely move through the orbit. This flow of chi is an automatic, though vital part, of the meditation. It may take a little getting used to resting the tongue at the roof of the mouth, but after a while it will seem second nature.

5. Close your eyes and move your awareness into the area about one inch behind the bridge of your nose and between your eyes. This area is about one-inch square and may be imagined as a kind of window. Some people say that the spot feels like a "comfortable little nest" while others have described it as kind of a "notch." Just find a place in this general area where it feels comfortable to rest your attention.

6. This is not concentration. It is focus. There should be no strain holding your awareness on this spot. Just let your attention rest in this area in a comfortable and easy way.

7. It does not matter if you have thoughts! Do not worry about your thoughts at all. Think of them as pigeons in a park. If you walk through an area of a park where there are pigeons, they will fly up all around you, making a lot of racket. But this will not deter you from walking. The same idea applies here. Thoughts and fantasies will float and sometimes storm around you. Don't fight them or judge them in any way. Just let them be there doing their thing. All you have to do is keep your focus or attention on this spot behind the nose and eyes. As long as you hold your attention here the meditation will work, even if you are thinking about something else!

If you have a timepiece, look at the time and try it for about five to ten minutes. When you look to see how many minutes have passed, sort of squint your eyes just enough to see. It is very important to slowly open your eyes at the end of the meditation, especially if you have gone "very deep."

How did you feel after you practiced this form?

What was your breathing pattern? Was it relaxed? Was it slower than before you started?

Do you feel a peaceful calm feeling?

Sometimes people also feel warmth or coolness or even tingling or other energy sensations in their bodies. All of this is natural and good. It is a sign that your body/mind system is re-balancing itself in a dynamic way.

Occasionally people have difficulty recognizing that they are more relaxed or that anything different has happened. If this is true for you, just stick with it for a while.

I suggest that you do this meditation form every day, at least once, for ten to twenty minutes. Twice a day would be even better. You can meditate, using this form, for as long as thirty minutes or even an hour. But twenty minutes, twice a day, will give you enormous benefits.

Below is a suggested Stress Management Program. It will not take much time from your day, and practiced on a regular basis, it will give you innumerable benefits including less tension, increased well-being, feelings of peace, and better health.

A Stress Management Program

1. Do the Two Minute Stress Buster three times in a row, pausing after each complete cycle and feeling your level of relaxation.
2. Sit comfortably with your legs out in front of you. Play

some soothing music that makes you relaxed and supports you to direct your attention "inward."

Close your eyes and do Noise Removal Breathing for two to three minutes.

Note your new level of relaxation.

3. Practice the Heaven's Gate Mediation for fifteen to twenty minutes.

This simple cycle of shifting brain states will take you about twenty to thirty minutes.

The ideal would be to do this sequence twice a day, once in the morning and once in the evening.

Give this Stress Management Program Protocol a go of it for at least thirty days. Don't miss a single day, and you will be amazed at the positive impact it will have on your performance, your energy, your health, and your relationships.

In this chapter, we have dealt with stress and how shifting brain states can help you reduce its effects. There is, however, one area we have not touched upon. It is one of the major factors that determine how stressful our reactions are to the events in our lives. And this crucial factor has to do with our style of dealing with stressful events.

Some of your current styles of dealing with stress may not be working for you, and may, in fact, be creating more stress in your life. Coping with problems through alcohol or drugs, by blaming others, or through depression are examples of coping styles that do not work.

Our personal styles of dealing with stress or disappointments are rooted in the personality and, ultimately, changing how we deal with stress must begin with changes in our attitudes towards ourself and others.

It is not in the scope of this book to address these most important issues; however, I have found an excellent resource in a book called *Super Immunity* by Paul Pearsall, Ph.D.

If you are a self-motivator, this book will give you a clear profile of how you respond to the stressors in your life, and how your coping style is affecting your health. In addition, Dr. Pearsall gives some excellent strategies to turn around your "negative" patterns of behavior into more "positive" and beneficial ways of coping.

This chapter may very well be one of the most important sections in this book. By using the exercises and practicing the techniques on a daily basis, you can transform your life and reach levels of performance that will amaze you.

There is, however, one requirement. *You must do it.* In the end, it is what we *do* that counts.

There is a double value in practicing these stress management techniques. Not only will they reduce the impact of stress in your life, they will also increase your awareness of your own "inner world." They will take you to a depth and richness that we rarely discover in the outer world of perception. And oddly, as we open these doors to our inner perception and its sense of peace and calm, our outer world becomes richer and more manageable.

As within so without.

CHAPTER NINE

The Inner Healer: Exploring the Ability to Self-Heal

"Here in this body are the sacred rivers; here are the sun and the moon as well as all the pilgrimage places... I have not encountered another temple as blissful as my own body."
— *Saraha*

D r. Inge Corless is nationally known for her work in nursing care for the terminally ill, especially persons living with AIDS. A professor and past chairperson of the Department of Secondary Care in the School of Nursing at the University of North Carolina, Dr. Corless is uniquely qualified to comment on the issues of healing.

One afternoon, she told me that she could think of situations in which patients had both been healed and physically died.

She described such patients as "dying well," that is with a sense of calm and without inner conflict. Healing for Dr. Corless is different than being cured.

A cure is a remission of disease. Healing involves the mental/

emotional and spiritual outlook of the person.

Although the processes of healing and remission are separate, healing can, sometimes, produce a cure. How this happens is not clearly understood, but we do have some idea of the mechanisms involved.

It is still considered heresy in some medical circles to consider that "the mind" or mental and emotional experiences can, in any way, affect physical processes such as disease.

Redford Williams, M.D., (*The Trusting Heart*) of Duke University has compared this deep-seated hostility to the idea of mental and emotional effects as a causative agent in disease to the rigidity of the Catholic Church when confronted with Copernicus's theory that the sun, and not the earth, was the center of the solar system.

The number of studies that explode the myth of the body as the only causative agent for health and disease is continually rising. Each year, it seems, new professional medical and research associations are forming to address newly emerging paradigms. It is as if a growing number of physicians and health professionals are recognizing that the old ways of viewing health and disease are too limited. Something new is needed.

For our purposes we can describe one of these new paradigms in this way:

It is possible, under certain conditions, to affect changes in the physical body through changes in mental and emotional experience.

The purpose of this chapter is to show you how to set up those "certain conditions." With the techniques in this section you can assist in your own healing and perhaps effect a cure as well.

Important Note: If you are currently experiencing the symptoms of an illness or disease, do not use these protocols in *lieu* of medical treatment. While these exercises can greatly accelerate healing, they are not a substitute for sound medical attention.

In a study conducted with heart attack patients, it was found that their sense of time affected the outcome of their treatment. Those patients who had a compressed sense of time, (not enough of it in other words) responded poorly to treatment and had a higher death rate than those persons who had a more expanded sense of time. This second group of patients felt easier about things and that somehow there would be more than enough time for them to accomplish what they wanted.

In other words, your sense of time may be, and probably is, affecting your health and well-being.

Time is plastic. It is not experienced the same in all situations. Have you ever been involved in something you really enjoyed only to discover that time had flown by? Conversely, have you ever been really bored with something and found each minute excruciatingly long? This is an example of time as a plastic medium.

Of course in each instance above, objective time, as measured by a clock, would be constant. But your subjective experience of time would speed up or slow down depending on a number of factors, including your interest.

One of the effects of the lower brain states is that our sense of time is altered. Time becomes more fluid. There is less internal pressure to get things done, and we feel a natural urge to lean back, relax, and let go.

This process of letting go of control has many positive effects as we discussed in the previous chapter on stress. It also allows us to experience the more creative impulses of the non-dominant hemisphere.

As an example, let me tell you about my first experience with self-hypnosis. At the time, I had been feeling some pressure and uncomfortable sensations in the area of my kidneys. Using the techniques of autohypnosis, I altered my own brain state and entered a relaxed and altered state of awareness.

Moving my attention into the area of my kidneys, I acted as if I could "talk" with them. I then asked them if they would communicate with me and tell me what I could do to get rid of the uncomfortableness.

Immediately, in my "mind's eye," I saw a trash truck and two trash men talking excitedly. They told me that the reason for the uncomfortableness was that I was eating too much junk food. To use their own words, "there is just so much junk we can haul away." They also advised me to drink more water.

I came out of that experience and cleaned up my diet. Within a few days, the uncomfortable sensations in my kidneys disappeared. And I learned a valuable lesson: I can talk to my body.

This idea may seem odd since we don't usually think of being able to communicate with our bodies. But in altered states of consciousness, there are possibilities for experiences that simply do not exist in our normal waking states of awareness.

The key is to alter your brain state, enter the more relaxed areas of Alpha and/or Theta, and then set up a protocol in which you "act as if" what you are experiencing is real. After the experience is over, you can analyze it to see what value, if any, the experience has for you. But it is vitally important to suspend your judgment during the actual experiences of altered states. Otherwise, your discriminating mind will enter and distort the information you are receiving.

The following protocol can be used for getting information from any system or area of your body.

Bodily Awareness Communication Protocol
  1. Put on the Creative Imagining tape mentioned earlier or play music you find relaxing and that supports you to

move your attention "inward."

2. Do Noise Removal Breathing for two to three minutes.
3. Do Level One Breathing.
4. Move your awareness into the area of your body with which you would like to communicate.
5. Imagine that this area can communicate with you. Some people may be able to see something or someone that represents this area or system. Others may hear a "voice" that talks to them, while others may have a felt sense of it. It is also possible to experience any combination of these.
6. Allow yourself to have a dialogue with this part of your body. As you communicate with this part, keep your inhales and exhales long, slow, and calm.
7. After you have finished, thank the part for having communicated with you.
8. Write down any of the suggestions that struck you as important and analyze them to discern their validity.

If you did not get anything when you went through this protocol, do not be discouraged. Keep working. Eventually you will be able to experience your body communicating with you. Using the above protocol, you may sometimes discover unusual circumstances or reasons for your problem.

I am reminded of an experience I had after my mother's death. She died during the spring, near Easter. Several years previously, I had gotten rid of a stubborn case of hay fever, and I had been symptom free ever since. Suddenly it came back with a vengeance. My eyes watered and burned, my nose stuffed up and ran constantly. I was miserable.

Using the method I just shared with you, I went "inside" and got in touch with the part of me that was having the hay fever reaction. Instantly, in front of me, a little boy appeared. He was me at about seven years old. He was very sad that he couldn't be with "mommy" anymore. He couldn't touch her anymore or hear her voice, and I somehow knew instantly that his grief had somehow affected my immune system. (Hay fever and other allergies are immune system reactions involving antigens or irritants.)

This image of my "inner child" self was, in my understanding, a representation of my feelings. I was not able, for various reasons, to feel the grief for the loss of my mother directly. My feelings had gone underground and were in some way affecting my immune function via the hypothalamic pathways in my brain.

As I experienced the image of my "inner child" and his sadness, I was overcome with my own and true feelings of grief. After crying for quite awhile, I imagined that I could take my "little boy" to a special place where he could see, touch, and hear my mother, his "mommy," again.

Shifting my brain state by altering my breathing pattern and by playing music that relaxed me, I slid into the relaxing state of Theta. I will never forget this experience.

The image of my mother appeared at the edge of a large meadow. As soon as I could see her, my "inner child" ran to her with tears of joy as he cried, arms reaching out, "mommy... mommy... mommy." I stayed in the meadow with the images of my mother and my "inner child" hugging each other for several minutes, and I cried again as feelings of loss mingled with feelings of peace.

I noticed, after this experience, that my hay fever symptoms disappeared for several days. They then returned again a lot less strongly. This was a very busy time for me, and so I did not take the time to go "inside" again. I tolerated the mild symptoms for a few more months until they finally left completely. In retrospect, I think I missed a wonderful opportunity to discover more about my own feelings and the workings of my brain and immunity.

There is another way to access communication with the body, and any of its organs or systems. This exercise can help you to get in touch with any "part" that might want you to be sick. It seems like an odd idea that a "part" of us might want us to be ill, but this is sometimes the case.

I once worked with a woman who had a series of rashes on her skin that were not responding to medical treatment. We discovered, in our work that she had a "part" that was "itching to be touched." Her problem went back to when she was a child and had been touch starved. The events in her adult life were bringing back those feelings and needs. She continued her medical treatment while also getting regular therapeutic massages and spending more time with her boyfriend just cuddling and touching. The symptoms decreased and eventually went away.

The next exercise is for gathering cognitive information, and people often get interesting and helpful answers to their questions. For example, at a psychoimmunology[1] seminar that my wife and I conducted several years ago, a woman was "told" by one of her breasts, during this protocol, that she had a lump needing attention. Upon going to her physician, she discovered that she had a very early form of breast cancer.

In this exercise you will be asked to write with both hands. The reason for this is that different hands access different areas of the brain. As the neural fibers from the brain enter the body, they switch sides. Thus the left side of the brain controls the right side of the body while the right side of the brain controls the left side of the body.

By writing with your non-dominant hand, you access areas of

---

[1] Psychoimmunology is the study of how mental and emotional experiences affect the body and immune system.

your brain you do not normally contact.

Writing from the Other Side of Your Brain

1. Put on the Creative Imagining tape mentioned earlier or play some music that you find relaxing and that supports you to move your attention "inward."
2. On a piece of paper, write out your question with your dominant hand (the hand with which you normally write.)
3. Pause and move your awareness into the area of the body or "part" you are asking the question of.
4. Without thinking about it, let your non-dominant hand write out an answer. (If you are right handed write out the answer with your left hand. If you are left handed, write out the answer with your right hand.
5. Continue to journal in this manner until you get the sense of an answer.

These first two protocols allow you to get cognitive information about your body, but there are deeper ways to reach healing than thinking. These deeper levels involve, as do all inner experiences, your sensory modalities.

Inner experiences, especially in low Theta, are experienced as real. The unconscious mind cannot distinguish between a real and an imaginary event. Thus, if you create a powerful healing experience in your mind, it can have vast and far reaching positive consequences.

This next exercise can produce powerful healing experiences, and in many cases it has helped to affect a "cure." It uses the image of what I call the "Inner Healer."

For some persons this may take the form of a shaman or witch doctor, while for others it may take the form of a powerful being or wise person. With people of the Christian faith, the Inner Healer often takes the form of Christ. Whatever image you feel comfortable with is the one that will work the best.

The Inner Healer is often a powerful and beautiful experience, and in addition to physical healing it can also be used for emotional healing as well.

The Inner Healer

1. Put on the Creative Imagining tape mentioned earlier or play some music that you find relaxing and that supports you to direct your attention "inward."
2. Sit comfortably and close your eyes. Do Noise Removal Breathing for two to three minutes.
3. Do Level One Breathing.
4. Imagine that you are in a beautiful open meadow or in a very special "healing temple." Choose an image that you are intuitively drawn to. Make the scene very real. See it, hear the sounds, and feel the physical sensation of your being there and the calm and peaceful emotions. Imagine that the air is filled with a sweet and pleasant aroma, breathe in this pleasing aroma. Spend several moments experiencing this scene as real while you breathe in the pleasant aroma.
5. Behind you, somewhere in this special place, is your Inner Healer. Turn and face him or her. In some instances, your Inner Healer may take the form of an animal. As you look at and sense your Inner Healer in front of you, get a feeling for his or her energy. Notice and feel the healer's great love for you. Rest in and feel this love for a few moments.
6. Go up to the Inner Healer and ask that you be healed of whatever it is you have come here for. It may be that you seek the healing of a physical illness or condition or emotional healing or just solace.
7. Allow the Inner Healer to work with you. Especially sense

the physical changes in your body and any sense of energy circulating or coming into you. The healer may also speak to you or advise you. Often these words can be of great value. Pay attention to them.

8. When the experience seems to be coming to a close, thank the Inner Healer for his or her help.

9. You can return to this "healing space" whenever you wish. If you have worked with it due to a particular illness or condition, it would be good if you worked with the exercise on a somewhat regular basis, perhaps once or twice a week.

The next protocol involves breathing and imaging. It is a very powerful exercise, and you can use it to direct healing energy to your entire body or to a specific area. I often do this exercise once or twice a week, and more if I'm feeling "worn down."

But before we go through the actual steps for the exercise, I would like to go over a little physiology.

There are basically two main sites for our immune system[2]: the thymus gland, located near the heart, and the bone marrow, that darkish substance in the center of bones. It is here in the bone marrow that new red blood cells are made, as well as the white blood cells and macrophages, which are essential to our immune function. The white blood cells and macrophages attack bacteria and other foreign bodies in our system.

The thymus gland manufactures t-Lymphocytes, another critical element in the arsenal of our defense against illness and invaders. Now, in children, the thymus is very large. But as we

---

[2] The lymph system is also an important element in the immune system. The lymph system is an extensive network underneath the skin. Some studies have shown that touching or stroking can positively affect immunity. It may very well be that the lymphatic system is responsible for some of these results.

grow older, the thymus gland starts to shrink, until in older adults it is often almost completely atrophied.

This exercise involves breathing an image of "light" into the thymus and bone marrow, and then directing it throughout the body. It is very relaxing and comforting.

Thymic Breathing

1. Put on the Creative Imagining tape mentioned earlier or play some music that you find relaxing and that supports you to direct your attention "inward."
2. Sit comfortably or lie down and close your eyes. Do Noise Removal Breathing for two to three minutes.
3. Imagine and feel that a beam of light is coming down from above and bathing your thymus and heart area in light. This light may be golden or white or some other color that you feel intuitively drawn to. It may even change color in the course of the exercise.
4. With each inhale draw the light into your thymus gland.
5. With each exhale let the light flow out of your thymus gland and into the bone marrow of your bones. Although the largest reservoirs of bone marrow in the body are the femurs or thigh bones, allow the light to move into all of your bones. Especially let the circulating light move into your spine. Stay with this breathing pattern for at least five to ten minutes.
6. If you have a specific area you wish to work with, draw the light into your thymus on the inhale, and let the light flow from your thymus to the area needing attention on the exhale. Do this for another five to ten minutes.
7. After you have finished this breathing pattern, just be with yourself for a few minutes, noting how you feel.

You can repeat this exercise as many times throughout the week as you wish. And you may also extend the breathing times past the five or ten minutes. It is a great way to relax and to increase feelings of well-being.

Our immune systems are exceedingly complex and sophisticated. Research and clinical observation continues to draw connections between immune function and emotions. And psychotherapeutic literature abounds with anecdotal reports of patients' ailments improving as the result of intensive inner work.

Until recently, measurable or quantifiable data on the effects of emotions on bodily functions and health were scant. However, that is all changing with the advent of computer topology and new sensing technologies.

One of the most exciting areas of research concerns the electromagnetic fields of the heart muscle. Several researchers, including psychophysiologist Dan Winter have developed a method of modeling the fluctuating electromagnetic fields of the heart in response to emotion.

In this view, the heart emits complex fields of energy that are directly affected by feelings. Emotions such as love actually make the energy fields more coherent (stronger), while emotions such as hatred and jealousy degrade the fields making them incoherent (weaker). As the coherent field of the heart expands through the emotion of love, it touches and enlivens other glands and organs of the body.

The research group at Heart Math Institute in Boulder Creek, California, has recently released data that measures increased DNA "braidedness" (order) in the presence of these coherent heart resonances.

In other words, how you feel affects your health.

Other researchers, no doubt, will replicate these studies. And this is as it should be. However, we need not wait to take advantage of this information.

Let's wean ourselves from destructive emotions such as fear, anger, hatred, and jealousy. They are, for the most part, with the exception of "valid" psychological responses, merely habits of responding. We can learn to respond in other more positive ways, and our health will be the beneficiary.

In the event of a serious illness, I strongly suggest professional psychotherapeutic support and regular use of the previous protocols in this chapter. However, it would be wise if we did not wait until we were sick to practice self-awareness. As the saying goes: "An ounce of prevention is worth a pound of cure."

Go through the previous exercises, and explore the interconnectedness of your body and mind. And should you "hear" your body talking to you, listen.

If you have an hour or so one afternoon or evening, you will find this final protocol very helpful, pleasing, and relaxing.

Mind/Body Healing Protocol
1. Play the Creative Imagining tape mentioned earlier or play some music that you find relaxing and that supports you to turn your attention "inward."
2. Sit comfortably or lie down, and close your eyes. Do Noise Removal Breathing for two to three minutes.
3. Do Level One Breathing.
4. Go through the Inner Healer Exercise.
5. After you have completed the Inner Healer, do the Thymic Breathing Exercise.
6. After you have completed the Thymic Breathing, imagine that you can smell one of your favorite aromas. With each inhale draw in this very pleasing smell. Breathe slowly and deeply, imagining that you can actually smell this

very satisfying aroma. As you exhale, let this pleasing aroma saturate your body so that the sweetness of this smell moves into every cell. Breathe in this way for three to five minutes.

7. Finally, let your breath return to its natural rhythm. Don't change it in any way. Just be aware of it. Notice the inhale and notice the exhale. Just be with your breath in this relaxing and comfortable way for a few minutes. As you continue to notice your breath, remember the feeling of love. That is, recall the feeling you have when you are loved or when you are loving someone or something. Let yourself breathe into this feeling. As you allow yourself to feel this emotion of love, you will be making the electromagnetic field of your heart more coherent. Take as long as you like to breathe and feel this emotion of love.

8. After doing this protocol, take a few minutes to be with yourself, before moving back into activity.

Managing Pain Through Awareness/Feedback

I liked Jocelyn from the moment I met her. A sensitive and accomplished artist, she very quickly learned how to access her deeper brain states. As a sophisticated world traveler, she had enjoyed numerous sojourns with her husband. However, her travels had been greatly reduced due to intractable rheumatoid arthritis.

She was often in constant pain, which, unfortunately, did not respond to pain killers.

Jocelyn came to see me on the advice of a friend. She was at her "wits end." She had "tried everything" and all allopathic medicine could do for her was to slow down some of the inflammation with cortisone shots.

In the course of our work together, we focused on some of the emotional issues that seemed to underpin her condition, and although there was some improvement, the greatest improvement came when I showed her how to use the awareness/feedback technique (AFT).

The concept of AFT is quite simple, and it is the opposite of what most of us do when we are in pain. Since pain is an unpleasant sensation, most of us use one of two methods for dealing with it: 1) we take a pain killer and 2) if we cannot get hold of a pain killer or it is not working, we try to put our attention on something else. This is understandable, but it deprives us of a very powerful ability of the brain/mind system, namely, to be aware of sensation and to alter it through feedback.

I taught Jocelyn a simple method of holding her focus on the painful sensations, of allowing her awareness to go into the center of the pain itself. As she focused on these intense sensations, they began to change. Sometimes they got more intense and started to burn. The burning sensations would then decrease until there was, miraculously, pleasure or no sensation at all! At times the pain would immediately decrease into a kind of pulsating sensation and then leave altogether. At other times the pain would move around in her body, slowly decreasing in intensity until it was gone.

Jocelyn got the hand of this technique quickly and reported to me that she was able to eliminate the most intense pain in her body through this method. Sometimes the pain would return, but with less intensity. She would then practice AFT again. This gave her innumerable benefits. She had control of her pain, and it helped to decrease her perception of being a helpless victim. This increase in her locus of self-control had other positive psychological benefits as well.

AFT did not stop the progression of her disease, at least as far as I know, but it did allow her to cope with it much more effectively.

According to Dan Winter, the psychophysiologist I mentioned in Chapter 8, using awareness in this manner can organically cure many "incurable" conditions such as cancer. The trick, according to Winter, is to hold awareness on the pain until it burns, and until the burning changes into comfortable sensation. Staying with this process in connection with increased emotional contact and improved nutrition has the potential to cure many conditions considered incurable. I have not personally seen such a remission with this method, however, I would not be surprised if I did. The reason I believe it is possible is that by focusing awareness on an area of the body in distress, we can activate the powerful internal healing mechanisms of the brain itself (which lie within the second level — hypothalamus, pituitary, limbic).

The actual neurological mechanisms involved in AFT remain to be clearly explained by science; however, whatever the mechanisms are, it appears to work!

The key point to remember with AFT is awareness. Focus your awareness on the pain itself. Go into the pain with your awareness, and "hang out" with the pain until it changes. Eventually it will alter, and at some point it will no longer be experienced as pain, but merely as sensation.

For some people doing AFT by themselves, the process of Image Streaming described in Chapter 10, may be helpful. Describe, in detail, everything about the pain. This process of description requires you to focus awareness on the pain itself, which is the central key to AFT.

If you choose to Image Stream your pain, describe such things as its color, shape, size, depth (is it just on the surface of your body, or does it seem to be deep inside?, etc.), and movement (does the pain pulse or whirl around or is it completely still?). Finally, if the painful sensation is moving describe the speed of its movement—fast, slow, or moderate. Go through this list over and over, describing, in detail, each aspect of the sensation until the pain decreases or disappears into comfortable sensation. This can take from a few seconds to several minutes.

If you are assisting someone in pain using this method, never actually use the word pain. Always use the word sensation. This is because words, themselves, have the power to program experience.

There are few mysteries of the body/mind that are more intriguing than our own immune systems. And the benefits of exploring this interconnectedness can be profound.

To know yourself is a key to both knowledge and power. To know and understand your immunity is to touch the inner sanctum of existence, the terra firma of "the mind" itself. For it is through our immune systems that we place the signature of our identity within our biology.

It is through our immune systems that we "know" and determine self from non-self.

The world cascades through our bodies in the form of molecules, bacteria, viruses, and a host of other "invisibles." As these visitors pass through us, it is our deepest biological sense of self that decides what to welcome and what to destroy.

To understand our immunity then, is to understand ourselves in the deepest and most intimate way. To become conscious of something so deeply embedded in the unconscious and automatic workings of our bodies is to wrestle free something of extraordinary value and worth.

It will take time for you to accomplish this. And it is not, generally speaking, an easy task. But the undertaking is, without a doubt, well worth the effort.

CHAPTER TEN

Increasing Intelligence, Creativity, and Language Abilities

"Sell your cleverness and buy bewilderment."
– Jalal Ud-Din Rumi

I ntelligence, though often equated with left hemispheric functions such as logic, language and sequencing ability, is actually much more complex. Howard Gardner, Ph.D., professor of psychology at Harvard University, has named eight different types of intelligence. They are:

1. Linguistic — the ability to use words
2. Mathematical/logical — the skill in reasoning and organization
3. Visual/spatial — abilities in patterning, imagery, and metaphor
4. Musical/auditory — skill with rhythm and musical patterning

5. Kinesthetic — physical and athletic skills
6. Inter-personal — skills in communication and sensitivity to others
7. Intra-personal — inner focusing skills and being able to work by yourself
8. Intuitive/spiritual — the skills to operate intuitively and to be aware of the dimensional aspects of consciousness

One of the tragedies of modern education is that, for the most part, it focuses on and rewards only two types of intelligence — linguistic and mathematical.

By over-focusing on language and math, we deprive our children and ourselves of developing other aspects of our intelligence. And, although it may not seem clear to you at present, our math and language abilities can be enhanced by developing other intelligences such as visual/spatial intelligence or through kinesthetic intelligence.

The modern world is putting untold pressures on us and our children. A twelfth-grade education was all it used to take to be successful. Now not even college is enough. We must make learning a lifetime proposition, otherwise we will not be able to keep up with the rapid changes exploding in almost every field of human endeavor and commerce. Our future happiness and economic opportunities will weigh heavily on how intelligent and valuable we become to both ourselves and others.

In this chapter, we will focus on proven methods to increase language ability, creativity, and other intelligence factors. While I agree that language and math abilities are important, I believe that the development of other intelligences are equally important. These other intelligences can actually increase our aptitude for language and math.

How, some might ask, can something as ephemeral as intuition improve our math and language abilities? The answer lies in the brain itself.

The third level in our information management system consists of our neocortex, which is divided into two distinct halves. These duplicate halves, called the left and right hemispheres, have distinctly different ways of perceiving the world, and are concerned with very different types of information.

While the left hemisphere is primarily verbal, the right hemisphere is non-verbal. The left is concerned with details, while the right is concerned with the whole. The left hemisphere is concerned with logic and sequence; the right, paradox and pattern. The right hemisphere is also musical and spatial. In some persons these are reversed, but with most people the left is verbal/logical and the right side is non-verbal/intuitive.

While further research has indicated that the brain is not as neatly divided up in this way as we once thought, there is nevertheless a tendency for the two cerebral hemispheres to operate in two very different contexts.

Now folded between the left and right hemispheres is a very important bundle of nerve fibers called the corpus callosum. It is through the corpus callosum that the left and right sides of the brain communicate with each other.

All mental activity and experience is processed via these two cerebral hemispheres. As a result, all of our mental impressions and choices are prejudiced via the side of our brain in which they are being processed.

In western industrialized cultures, the experiences and functions of the left, or dominant hemisphere, are the most rewarded. After all, it is our intellect which has allowed us to create science and technology.

The experiences characteristic of the right hemisphere have largely been disregarded. They have, for the most part, been considered as too way out, impractical, or other worldly. But this prejudice is based on a gross misunderstanding of the non-dominant hemisphere's function and possibilities.

Information from the non-dominant hemisphere is responsible for many of our greatest advances in science and technology. Albert Einstein conceived of the General Theory of Relativity by fantasizing about trains and rockets. The structure of the benzene ring in chemistry was discovered by a chemist dreaming a dream in which a snake was eating its own tail. Dreams and fantasies are experiences that are largely generated by the non-dominant hemisphere.

Have you ever had the experience of trying to describe a dream only to find that your description sounded hollow and was unable to come close to the compelling depth and richness of the actual experience? Dreams, like other deep human emotions, cannot be captured in words. We know that language is based in processes involving, for most people, the left cerebral hemisphere. Two sites and a multitude of neural connections make language possible. Communication via language involves complex flows of neural information from many areas of the brain into the language and speech centers.

Let me give you an example.

Recall a pleasant feeling, and for a few moments just enjoy that pleasurable feeling. Get this feeling before you go on to the next paragraph.

If I were to ask you to tell me what you felt, you might say "I felt a pleasant feeling." But please note that the verbal communication "I felt a pleasant feeling" is quite different from the actual experience of feeling something pleasant. The verbal communication is an abstraction that can never capture the essence of the experience. Now, it is neurologically possible to experience pleasure without ever being able to put that experience into words. This is because the pleasure centers in the brain are not directly connected with our language centers. Thus it is possible to experience something strongly (like pleasure), but have no adequate words to describe it. The process of describing an experience involves the connecting of different and divergent areas in the brain.

People often have experiences or hunches about things that they can't put into words. This is because the brain's language centers have not been "trained" to translate impressions from the non-dominant hemisphere. The reason in most cases is that the corpus callosum is not able to (or is simply untrained to) connect the information from both hemispheres.

By training the language centers to translate impressions from the non-dominant hemisphere into words, a remarkable thing happens. Language ability increases and so do other intelligence factors such as problem solving ability and, it seems, some aspects of measurable Intelligence Quotients (IQ).

(Intelligence Quotients are currently the topic of immense controversy in educational circles because they only measure very limited areas of intelligence and are, for the most part, culturally biased. Nevertheless, some of the processes in this chapter tend to increase certain types of IQ measurement.)

The process of translating impressions into language was pioneered by Dr. Wenger in a process he calls "Image Streaming." I mentioned Wenger earlier in this book, identifying him as an expert on genius and intelligence. When you practice the technique of Image Streaming, you will see for yourself that this accolade is well deserved. (For further information about Dr. Wenger and Project Renaissance, see Appendix C).

In a couple of independent studies, Image Streaming has been documented to increase intelligence factors such as problem solving abilities and language proficiency. In terms of measurement, it was found that the IQ of some individuals went up one point for approximately every eighty minutes of usage.

The exercise uses something called "the inner witness." This inner witness is a function of your higher cortical brain areas and allows you to be aware of yourself experiencing an event — not just experiencing the event, but aware of yourself experiencing the event.

It may seem odd, at first, to describe *out loud* your inner experiences, but it is the actual process of description that increases both intelligence and language abilities in this exercise.

The exercise is quite easy to do, and it is entertaining as well. The protocol is described below. It is important to follow the instructions exactly as written.

Image Streaming Protocol

1. Put on the Creative Imagining tape. (See Appendix B.) If you do not have this tape, you can use any music that helps you to relax and turn "inward." You can also do this exercise without music, if you wish.

   Note: The Creative Imagining tape was specifically created to enhance the Image Streaming process. It will evoke many different types of experiences including fantasies, visual images, or physical sensations. Normally we do not describe these types of things. But by describing every detail of your inner experience, you will make linkages between the language part of your brain and other areas, specifically the non-dominant hemisphere. It is this linkage that stimulates the increase in intelligence.

2. Sit comfortably and close your eyes.

3. Imagine that you have a tape recorder in front of you. Describe into this imaginary tape recorder every minute detail of what you are experiencing. If you are having a fantasy, describe it. If you see something, describe everything about it — its shape, color, etc. If you feel a physical

sensation, describe everything about it. Even if the images and feelings do not make logical sense to you, describe everything about them.

4. Continue this description of your inner experience for approximately twenty minutes. The more you practice this exercise, the more rapid will be your advancement.

For best results, do this exercise for twenty minutes a day, several times a week. You will be quite amazed at the increases in your ability to express yourself and to communicate more effectively.

Many of our greatest inventors and scientists have had remarkable visualization abilities. Albert Einstein was able to imagine pictures of real and imagined events in his mind. Nikola Tesla was said to have rotated three dimensional pictures of machines and inventions in his mind, to look for trouble spots. The late writer and engineer Itzak Bentov also had this ability to "see" with his "mind's eye."

Anecdotal research has indicated that most people (including some blind persons) process visual information whether or not they have conscious access to internal visual images.

Persons who consciously process internal visual information are good "visualizers." They can "see" in their "mind's eye" real or imagined objects and scenes. In more advanced visualization abilities a person can actually rotate an imaginary object in space and see aspects or details that were hidden from the front view.

It is possible for any sighted person, and some blind persons, to develop and/or increase their visualization abilities. It is important to remember that you already visualize, even if you cannot, at present, do it consciously.

The following protocol, if used faithfully, will develop your visualization abilities, or if you already visualize, it will greatly increase your abilities.

Visualization Development Exercise

1. Find a color picture, preferably one that captures your imagination. Place the picture in front of you and play the Creative Imagining tape or some other kind of relaxing music at low volume. As you look at the picture, describe to yourself in minute detail every detail of the picture as you look at it. What are the colors, shapes? Take a good five minutes to look at and describe every detail. The more details you notice and describe, the more effective the exercise will be.

2. After you have completed this part of the exercise, close your eyes with the tape still playing. Now imagine the picture in front of you, and begin to describe what you "see" in your "mind's eye." If it seems that you do not see anything, repeat your earlier verbal description (when you had your eyes opened). As you go through your description you may begin to sense subtle visual impressions, as if you can almost see in your imagination what you are describing out loud. (Note: You may notice, during this part of the exercise, subtle sensations in the area of your forehead. If this occurs, just enjoy them and continue with your description.)

3. After you have worked with re-creating a visual image of the picture in your "mind's eye," begin to imagine that the picture is a three dimensional image. Imagine yourself moving through this three dimensional world, and feel/sense what this would be like. Imagine looking at objects from different angles and different sides.

Most non-visualizing people require several attempts at the exercise before they start to "see" internal visual images. Be patient and have fun with the exercise. Remember that you already process visual images beneath the level of your conscious mind and by relaxing into the music and by describing the picture, both real and imagined, you bring into conscious awareness those visual images. This process will give you the ability to visualize or greatly enhance your already existing ability.

In this next section, we will look at how you can increase your intelligence by making minute physical changes within your own brain.

In the arrogance and narcissism of our own minds, we can easily forget that our desires and most aspiring ideas are fabricated from neural connections inside our skulls. The lofty heights of our own Pegasus are rooted in and limited by the physical integrity of about four pounds of flesh.

The brain makes thought possible due to its almost limitless capacity for hooking up nerve cells. This process of intercommunication involves two primary functions: oxygenation and neural networking.

Let's take oxygenation first.

The brain is an oxygen addict. It consumes oxygen in large quantities because without this colorless gas, it will die within minutes. The brain has an elaborate system of arteries, veins, and capillaries to insure the feeding and nourishing of its almost 100 billion neurons.

If it could be possible to increase the level of oxygenation within the brain itself, there would be an increase in brain function and potential.

As an example, imagine a clogged carburetor or fuel injector on your automobile. If you clean out the clog, your engine will get more oxygen, the firing inside the pistons will be cleaner, and your car will have more horsepower.

The injector of oxygen inside your brain, to use this analogy, is the network of capillaries that feed each of your myriad brain cells. The pistons are the mitochondria or power stations inside each cell. If the capillaries are clear and oxygen flows through them easily, the mitochondria will be able to produce more "cell power." And the result of several billion nerve cells being oxygenated at higher levels translates into much greater "mind power."

One method of enlarging the capillary network within your brain involves swimming underwater. The great Japanese inventor Yoshiro Nakamats, Ph.D. attributes part of his phenomenal creativity to underwater swimming. Dr. Nakamats invented the folding landing gear for airplanes when he was still a child, and later he invented the floppy disk that revolutionized the computer industry. He is credited with more patents than Thomas Edison and is a prodigious thinker.

From early on, Dr. Nakamats developed the habit of swimming underwater. He swims to the deeper parts of a swimming pool where he sits and contemplates underwater. He even has a special metal pad and pen so he can make notes on ideas that occur to him.

The act of holding your breath and swimming underwater stimulates capillary development in your brain. But you need not be as esoteric as Dr. Nakamats in your underwater swim. Simply swimming underwater for several minutes at a time and increasing the duration slowly over days and weeks will greatly add to your brain's oxygen capacity.

Aerobic exercise is another way to increase oxygenation of the brain. I had a very personal experience with this method and can vouch for its effectiveness. Several years ago I was involved with the administration of a small international company. It was an extremely stressful time. In addition to sixty-eighty hour weeks, I traveled quite often to the West coast and to Hong Kong to conduct trainings. The drain on my energy was incredible.

I stopped exercising due to the time crunch. After several months of this stress, I noticed that my attention was not as good as it had been. My mind felt slower.

I took up an aerobic exercise program and made the time to exercise on a regular basis. In just a few weeks, my mind felt sharper and clearer. I had, no doubt, increased the oxygenation of my brain's neural network through regular vigorous exercise.

It is the networking of thousands upon thousands of nerve cells that gives our thought and emotion its power. By stimulating the interconnecting or networking of neurons, we can greatly increase our brain power. But the neurological foundation for creative thinking and intelligence does not begin, as you would think, in the neocortex.

When I recently visited a friend, whose baby was learning to crawl, I was fascinated by how he pulled himself across the room, belly to the floor like some kind of half-snake.

A few weeks later when I dropped by to say hello, Jesse had learned to pull himself off the floor onto all fours and could scoot around the room at quite a clip. I noticed a classical movement that is repeated in most human babies as they learn to crawl on all fours. As he moved his left arm out, his right leg came in, and as he pulled himself forwards, his right arm would come out as his left leg came in. The motion is called cross-crawling. And if a child is confined too much, and not allowed to crawl in this way, it can have untold ramifications on his ability to learn.

Somehow this movement, which requires a coordination of the right and left brain's motor areas, develops a platform for future neurological connections in the cerebral cortex, or third level.

Although most of the standard strategies for increasing intelligence are based in changing our mental functions, it is possible to increase some areas of intelligence by using the body. I have seen remarkable improvements in mental function in persons who were trained to cross-crawl, especially if they never learned it as children.

One way adults can recapture this early movement in themselves, and thereby stimulate those motor areas of their brains, is through a technique called Educational Kinesiology.

Educational Kinesiology or EduK is a system of educating the brain through movement. It is a synthesis of several techniques and was formulated and promoted by Paul Dennison, Ph.D. an educator with a background in Learning Differences (LD). I have seen some rather remarkable results with EduK. By stimulating a reorganization of first and second level information processes in the brain, such diverse areas as reading, concentration, and co-ordination can be improved. You will find information on how to contact the EduK Foundation in Appendix C.

The stimulating of new neural connections in the brain is still a rather controversial area of neurology. But more and more research is verifying that the brain's neural networks can be stimulated into making new linkages.

There is an extraordinary example of this in the field of geriatrics. For years it was assumed that age meant an irreversible decline in mental and physical ability. The culmination of this belief is the nursing home, where older citizens are carted off to wait for death. With all of their needs taken care of, most patients become lethargic, passive, and uninterested in their environment.

Anecdotal research from many places is showing that our concept of aging is a gross misconception. In one study with elderly men, it was found that they could add lean muscle mass to their bodies through regular weight training. We are also recognizing that creativity and mental capacity can actually *increase* with age. The key is stimulation.

If the brain is stimulated by the environment it will continue to grow and learn. If it is not stimulated by the environment, it will shut down, turn within, and become passive.

All you have to do is walk into the average nursing home and see why so many of the patients are passive and uninterested in the world around them. There is virtually no mental stimulation.

Anyone wanting to remain as mentally active and as "sharp" as possible would be well advised to keep themselves stimulated and interested in things around them. The old adage use it or lose it is quite appropriate when discussing the brain and "the mind."

No matter how old you are, no matter what your background, your brain can be stimulated to grow and to learn.

Using Dr. Gardner's eight classifications of intelligence, one could create a program of brain enrichment for themselves.

If, for instance, you are interested in increasing your linguistic intelligence, learn a new language or learn how to write poetry. If you want to increase your mathematical intelligence, learn algebra or geometry for the fun of it.

Want to increase your kinesthetic intelligence? Then learn one of the martial arts, Tai Chi, or a new sport. Don't let the myth that you are too old to take up physical activity hold you back.

Interested in expanding your musical intelligence? Learn how to play a musical instrument. To increase your visual and spatial intelligence take up one of the fine arts like painting, drawing, or sculpture.

If you want to increase your intuitive or spiritual intelligence, take up one of the many meditation forms and begin to explore your own consciousness.

By increasing your intelligence in as many areas as possible, you increase your likelihood of a richly rewarding life.

Actually this concept is not new. It formed the central motivating idea behind liberal arts education in which all areas of human endeavor were emphasized. The idea was that a well-rounded individual would be of more value to himself or herself than someone who was totally focused just on his or her area of expertise.

Unfortunately, this idea in education is becoming somewhat of an anachronism.

On Creativity

In my practice, I am often consulted by persons who wish to increase their creative abilities. It is something that is desperately desired by many people because they recognize that creativity is their passkey to a better life — either for job advancement or for a richer sense of themselves.

Creativity is one of the most illusive of abilities, yet it is quite simple. Creativity is the ability to sense and imagine things in new ways.

Once during a creativity and genius training session, I turned all of the chairs on their sides before the participants came into the room. As the attorneys, engineers, scientists, and other professionals came into the training area I watched their actions. Each one of them (except for one) turned their chairs upright and sat in them, certainly a most appropriate thing to do.

However, when I did the same thing with a group of four-, five-, and six-year-olds, it was quite a different story. Some of these young people turned their overturned chairs into imaginary castles or ships at sea searching for treasure. This is creativity in action.

Adults, for the most part, have had their creativity educated out of them. Gone are the attitudes of discovery and curiosity. A child will often do something just to see what will happen, while most adults won't try something new unless they know what will happen. What a tragedy that we have become imprisoned in the walls of such utter stupidity.

Now, I am not suggesting that you go out and turn your chairs over and pretend that you are in an imaginary place — at least not in public. But I do suggest that you start to free yourself from the known and enter the unknown, not with trepidation, but with curiosity and discovery. To borrow an ancient adage — Except ye be as little children, ye cannot enter the kingdom of creativity.

What do I mean by this?

When those successful professionals entered the training room and turned their chairs right side up, they were doing two things. They were being appropriate, and they were doing what was expected. Doing what is expected is the death knell to creativity.

Creativity requires a plasticity or flexibility of perception. And lest you think this has no practical implications, let me tell you a little story.

Before the 1970s, Switzerland was the heart of watch manufacturing worldwide. It held 80 percent of the market share, and time pieces were synonymous with the Swiss.

Near the beginning of the '70s, a Swiss inventor at one of the Swiss watch companies discovered a new way of telling time. It did not involve any moving parts. It operated on batteries instead of springs. When he took his idea to the company, they laughed at him. They said that his idea was not a watch at all. They had become so accustomed to looking at keeping time in one particular way that they were unable to conceive of it in any other form.

The short of the story is that the idea was never protected by a patent, and it was snatched up by the Japanese and a new company called Texas Instruments. The digital watch was born, and since then the Swiss have lost more than fifty percent of their market share. They had a gold mine in their hands, and they never knew it.

Those company officials simply did not have the plasticity or flexibility of perception to see the concept of a watch in new ways. Their lack of creativity cost them, and the Swiss economy, billions of dollars.

The ability to stretch our perception and see more than our learned view of things is not only creative, it is becoming a necessity in our fast-paced world economy.

So how then can we make our perception more plastic, more flexible? The method lies, once again, in the brain itself.

Creativity involves three separate levels: perception, feeling/intuition, and thinking/imagination.

Let me give you an example of this process from the biography of one of America's greatest financiers, Harvey Firestone. It was Mr. Firestone's desire to make the best tires he was capable of and deliver the best service to his customers. As his company grew larger and more successful, he followed the standard ideas on how to run a business. He had vice-presidents and hundreds of middle management employees. But he had a problem. The company had grown so large no one knew what was really happening. His vice presidents were regularly sent reports from all of the company's various departments, but they were too large to read. As a result, much of the company was operating in the dark. Firestone had an uneasy feeling that things were not what they should be even though the company was prospering and by all measurements was extremely successful.

When the stock market crash of the '20s hit, Firestone, like many of the country's larger companies, had a hard time of it. He immediately put a radical plan into action. It called for a departure from the standard wisdom on how to run a company. He decided that he, and he alone, would have to be responsible for the company. If something went wrong with a tire, it was not the problem of the worker, but the problem of that worker's manager. Firestone got rid of middle management. The vice presidents were reduced from dozens to one, directly accountable to the president.

The company's paperwork was drastically reduced, and reports were kept short and to the point so that the president and vice president knew what was happening.

The result was that Firestone not only survived the crash, but thrived during the depression.

Firestone's creativity saved his company. He was able to go beyond the known and approved ways of running a company. His thinking was plastic and flexible enough to imagine new ways of doing old things.

We can outline Firestone's management of information in this way: Firestone perceived a problem in his company that led him to the uneasy feeling that something was wrong, even though he couldn't quite put his finger on it. (This is a classic right brain/left brain dichotomy. The right brain has perceived something but is unable to put it into words). Eventually, Firestone was able to describe the problem to himself and, through imaginative thinking, he was able to come up with new ways of running his business. His actions saved not only his company but the jobs of hundreds of employees as well.

The fastest way I know to increase your creativity is to develop the areas of perception, feeling/intuition, and thinking/imagination.

Perception

Develop your five senses. Let yourself luxuriate in sensory impressions as you go about your day. Don't, for example, just lay your calendar on the desk. Feel its texture as you put it down. Notice pleasant aromas. They are powerful brain boosters. Surround yourself by beauty such as art or flowers. Beautiful objects and environments stimulate the brain. To heighten your sensory intelligence go through the protocol at the end of this chapter.

Feelings/Intuition

There are two kinds of feelings in regard to creativity. One set of feelings is called intuition. It is basically the "felt sense" of a situation or idea. It usually comes as a hunch or fleeting feeling.

People often overlook their intuitive hunches because hunches do not appear to be rational thoughts and seemingly have no justification.

But remember that intuition is a function of the non-verbal hemisphere, and therefore it does not have language as part of it. However, we can learn to translate our intuitive feelings into words, though the words, of course, can never actually capture the feeling. Processes of description, such as Image Streaming are one of the best methods for learning how to translate intuitive impressions into language. This process allows you to get a handle on the more ephemeral and hard to grasp intuitive feelings.

While the process of description allows us to better understand our intuitive feelings, the actual process of intuition is based in sensory impressions. To describe this process I must digress for a moment and describe the process of sensing itself.

Let's take one of the senses, say sight. To do this exercise, you will need something beautiful to put in front of you such as a flower or a piece of sculpture or some other object you find pleasurable. If you have the Creative Imagining (See Appendix B), put it on at low volume. Sit comfortably and gaze at the object you have chosen.

For description's sake, let's say that you have chosen a pink flower. As you look at the flower, notice its color and then notice that there are actually myriads of colors. Instead of just pink, there are many hues of pink with hints of different colors in different areas of the petals. Now begin to shift your brain state by doing Noise Removal Breathing for about two or three minutes as you continue to look casually at the flower. After you finish the breathing protocol, let your breath be long, slow and even. Continue to breathe in this relaxing manner as you look at the edges of the flower. Notice the subtle changes in the surface and edges of the petals. Notice again the subtle differences in color. Notice as many details of the flower as possible, all the while continuing to breathe in this comfortable and relaxed manner.

What at first appeared to be just a pink flower is now seen to be a complex assemblage of subtle differences in color, shading, and shape. This ability to sense subtlety is the stuff out of which intuition emerges. By training yourself to notice the subtle differences between things, you can greatly increase your intuitive abilities. Pay attention to people's voices, for example, and you will be able to hear things in them that are never said, but that are, nevertheless, there. Emotions such as fear or jealousy or confusion, or the sound of a child's voice in the body of an adult are just a few examples of what can be "read" in a voice when you pay attention to the subtle details.

For most people, attention to subtlety is not a conscious process. Thus subtle nuances may more likely be picked up by the non-dominant, non-speaking hemisphere. The result will be that the person may have an intuitive feeling about a situation but not know the reason why. Developing your ability to notice subtleties will greatly increase your conscious and unconscious intuitive abilities.

I said that there are two classes of feelings in relation to creativity. We just discussed the first one, intuitive feelings. The second class of feelings are more likely to be described as emotions.

The release of creativity can often generate powerful feelings. It is ironic that people who come to me to open their creative potential sometimes find themselves face to face with fear when it starts to emerge.

I recall a client who came to see me because he had been offered early retirement. He had hated his job for years and had often felt that he would be happier doing something else. When his opportunity came, he was paralyzed with fear. As we worked with the emotional issues around enjoying himself, a great wave of creativity emerged. He looked ten years younger, and he was suddenly filled with energy and enthusiasm. The change briefly scared him. After all, what would he do with this much energy? He reported, as have many clients, that he felt scared at feeling so good.

I believe that our fears of increased creative power go back to our childhood. Children are exuberant dynamos of creative energy. The process of education and socialization, though perhaps necessary, takes a heavy toll. We learn to be still, to be quiet, to be appropriate. Eventually these messages become internalized as powerful censors on our own perception and experience. When we are suddenly filled by the emotions of released creativity, it is only natural to want to dance, to sing, to jump around as kids. But the censor, inherited from our years of growing up, steps in and tells us to "be quiet, still, and appropriate." The result is often a tug of war between the self that wants to sing and dance and the self that wants to be a perfect adult (whatever that is).

If you find strong emotions surfacing into your awareness as you open your creativity, you may find some of the exploratory protocols in the section called Multiple Selves (Chapter 11) helpful.

Thinking and Imagination

I would not presume to give you any advice on how to think creatively in such a small space as this chapter. Rather, I would refer you to some of the excellent programs and resources on the subject. (See Appendix C.)

As to imagination, I would say take time to be a child again and pretend. One of the best ways to learn imagination is to hang out with young children. They naturally have vivid imaginations. In the area of imagination, you have a lot to learn from a four-year-old.

In addition, the following two protocols will help you lay the neurological groundwork for your own increased imagination through attention to the brain's sensory based maps.

Besides educating your brain in the powers of sensory based imagination, the exercises are fun to do.

A Protocol to Increase Sensory-Based Intuition

1. Olfactory-based exercise

Get together four to six different aromatic substances such as a slice of lemon, pineapple, a slice of orange, papaya, ground cinnamon, banana, cloves, strawberries, basil, eucalyptus, vanilla extract, mustard.

Lay them out on a table and, sitting comfortably, play the Creative Imagining tape in the background at low volume. If you don't have this tape you can play music that you find relaxing and that supports you to turn your attention inward.

If you are doing this with a partner (it's more fun this way), have him or her hold the substances up to your nose while you close your eyes. Go through each of the aromas. The idea is not to name the smell, although the analytical part of your mind may do this automatically. Let your awareness be on the texture of the smell itself. Sense the subtle differences between the aromas and feel where they seem to stimulate your nose and sinuses.

After you have gone through each of the smells, go through them again in your mind. Imagine that you can re-create the smell by remembering what it smells like. After you have gone through each one in your imagination, go back through it again for real. You may want to go through each one this way. For instance, smelling vanilla in your imagination and then smelling it for real, followed once more by your imagination. Go through all the aromas in this way.

Next, pick your favorite aroma out of all the ones you tried. With your eyes closed, begin to do the Noise Removal Breathing as you breathe in the favored smell. Do this for at least two to three minutes. As you breathe in this way, notice any sensory impressions, memories or feelings that come to your awareness. Describe these impressions, memories and feelings in the form of Image Streaming as discussed previously.

When I first practiced this part of the exercise, I used mustard. Suddenly, as I breathed in the aroma, I found myself back in fourth grade unwrapping my bologna and cheese sandwich. I even felt the texture of the wax paper. Smell is a powerful catalyst for memory and feeling.

Practicing this protocol on a regular basis will stimulate your brain in untold ways, increasing your acuity to subtle sensory signals, especially smells.

Multiple Sensory Exercise
1. Place a glass of water on a flat surface in front of you. Play the Creative Imagining tape, if you have it, or some other kind of music that supports you to relax and turn your attention inward.
2. Very slowly raise the glass to your lips and take a sip of the liquid. Look at your hand holding the glass and watch the

glass as you lift it off its resting place and raise it towards your face. Feel the glass against your lips. Feel the texture of the glass in your hand, the smoothness or its roughness. Feel the coolness or the warmth of the container. As you look at it, sense the shape of the glass and its edges in your hand.

3. Now put the glass back down and close your eyes. Do Noise Removal Breathing for a few minutes. Continuing to let your breath be slow and calm, imagine that you are holding the glass in your hand and raise it to your lips. Don't actually raise your hand, just imagine yourself doing it. Imagine seeing the glass, feeling it in your hands, feeling it against your lips, tasting the liquid, and swallowing it.

4. Repeat the exercise by going back through step #2 and then through step #3.

This protocol exercises the imaginative faculty by calling on a specific use of sensory detail. You can use the exercise with other objects as well. The idea is to re-create in your mind what you actually do with the object. Attention to detail is a must for the exercise to be successful.

In this chapter, we have looked at how you can increase your intelligence, creativity, and language abilities. The key to all of this is practice. If you don't actually go through the protocols on a regular basis you will not be training your brain to perform in this manner. It will just be another bunch of useless ideas in your head. Use these exercises, however, and you will discover a richness to your mental life that you cannot now imagine.

CHAPTER ELEVEN

Talking Heads and the Multiplicity of Selves

"When an inner situation is not made conscious,
it appears outside as fate."

– Carl Jung

A my was an attractive, vibrant, and sensitive woman in her early thirties. She had been recently laid off from her position in a large corporation due to scaling down, and the sudden change in her lifestyle had left her with an intractable depression.

She was married with three children. Frustrated with corporate life, she had started a consulting job, but things were not going well. She reported to me that she could not concentrate the way she used to, nor attend to the myriad details that her new undertaking demanded.

The depression had gone on for about six months when she came in to see me. She did not feel confident that her depression could be turned around since other attempts had failed. She was reluctant to take medication.

One thing struck me immediately from the start. Amy had two sides to her. One side was the immaculate housekeeper, the highly successful business person, and the social philanthropist. Amy had a well-deserved reputation as a person who made things happen. She served on several non-profit boards, coordinated large corporate gifts to different charities, and headed many fund drives.

I admired this attribute of Amy's and told her so during her first visit. It was right at that very moment, that Amy's other side showed her face. My compliments, meant to put her more at ease, made her very uncomfortable. I had the very odd sensation, in that moment, that some part of her was actually recoiling from my words.

This part of her I called "the other Amy." This other self was the source of Amy's depression. Her current problems were not due to the change in her job situation, although the stress of them had set the stage. The source of Amy's depression actually went back some thirty years earlier.

In the course of our work, it became very clear that Amy had come from a destructive, unloving, and uncaring family. The depth of her childhood pain was staggering, and I am still haunted by an early childhood memory she shared with me that illustrated the depth of her pain.

To Amy, it was as if it had happened yesterday. The memory was vivid, every detail intact.

She was three or four years old and had wandered onto a bridge in her backyard. The bridge crossed over a large stream that had recently flooded its banks. The rushing water had pulled the foundation of the bridge loose from the other bank, and the small wooden bridge hung precariously over the turbulent water. As Amy stood on the bridge, she watched the stream rushing beneath her and wished that the stream would carry her away. Transfixed in her childhood experience, she thought that death was like a stream that could carry her away from this hurtful world as well.

Just at that moment, Amy heard her mother frantically calling out to her. For a moment, Amy struggled with a deep and inner turmoil. Her mother was calling her, but the stream was calling her as well. One voice called her back into a world of pain and humiliation. The other called her into the release of death.

Amy still doesn't know why she came back into the yard off the bridge. Perhaps the fear of her mother brought her back into life.

This early critical incident made such an impact on Amy that she often had dreams about it, and she could call it up in clear and vivid detail some thirty years later.

Amy's early struggle to jump from the bridge or come back into life had set the stage for her depression. For you see, Amy had another self, a much younger self than the mature woman who came into my office once a week. This younger Amy had precious few resources. To her, the world was so unbearable and painful that the only recourse left was to take her own life.

Without the crutch of Amy's business demands, "the other Amy" came crashing into her awareness. Every day had become a battle between these two very real selves. One wanted to live and make a contribution to the world. The other wanted to die and be done with it.

These two selves were perfectly matched with equal psychological strength.

My goal in the work was to empower "the other Amy" with more resources to deal with her pain and to empower the adult Amy to more effectively manage the other destructive self.

It is not in the course of this book to explain how we accomplished our goals, but after about ten weeks of treatment, Amy was out of her depression and functioning much better. She began pulling together her consulting business. This was accomplished using the power of brain states, without having to resort to medication.

I believe that one of the reasons for the success of our work together was that we acknowledged "the other Amy," the other destructive self, as real.

Another reason for our success was Amy's deep and abiding faith in God. This faith, I observed, helped her weather the difficult psychological passages our work entailed.

(Note: There is a significant amount of research that implicates religious faith as a factor in mental health. It seems that any type of faith in a "supreme being" or "a higher order" has positive benefits in terms of psychological adaptation.)

With a rise in the diagnosis of multiple personality disorders, the idea of a multiplicity of selves has recently received more serious attention by the therapeutic community.

The idea behind a multiplicity of selves is quite simple. There is no "one self" at all, but rather many selves that weave in and out of our awareness.

For instance, have you ever been in a bad mood, a state of mind in which nothing is positive? This is an example of "another self." This other self has a psychological life all its own, and all it takes is the right set of circumstances for it to take over. Many a spouse has experienced their mate going into such a mood, and experience eventually teaches them to leave their loved one alone until they come out of it. Trying to cheer someone up when they are lost in the grips of a negative self (or mood) is like pouring water in to a bucket with holes in the bottom.

I called this chapter Talking Heads because many people

experience their other selves as voices that actually talk to them. This was true for Amy. Whenever "the other Amy" was around, she would make negative comments about what the adult Amy was trying to do.

It used to be that if a person heard voices, it was a virtual guaranteed diagnosis of psychosis or schizophrenia. This is still the case with some less enlightened mental health professionals. But research in the area of NLP (NeuroLinguistic Programming) has clearly shown that all people are biased in their sensory experience.

Some persons, called auditory learners, do actually hear voices in their heads, and it has absolutely nothing to do with mental illness. It is simply the way they store information. My sense is that the signature of possible mental illness is not so much whether a person "hears" voices or not, but is rather determined by what those voices say, what they would have the person do, and whether the person's behavior is affected or not.

Other people, called kinesthetic learners, store information by getting a felt sense about it. For these people a change in self is experienced as a sudden and intense shifting of emotion.

Visual learners, those who store information by making pictures in their heads, sometimes see visions when another self comes into their awareness. This is especially true if the person is in an altered state of awareness at the time.

The most obvious area of human psychology where the multiplicity of selves is evident is with Multiple Personality Disorders (MPDs).

These persons have two or more distinct selves that are autonomous and have very unique personalities that often are not aware of each other. For instance, one client had three different selves with very different behaviors. This made for a very confusing situation.

One of the selves liked to shop, another liked to save money. When she was in her "saving self" she put money aside. But periodically her bank account would empty, and she would have merchandise she had never seen before all over the apartment. Unknown to her, another self had gone out and compulsively spent her hard earned money.

EEG studies of MPDs have shown that each of their alternate selves has a very unique brain wave patterning profile. These alternate selves may even have allergies or phobias that the primary or root self does not experience. The ramifications of this are staggering. It would be as if a person brought in for finger-printing was found to have two or more sets of prints that changed under varying circumstances.

I think that, over the next few years, psychologists will come to a much deeper understanding of MPDs, and this understand-ing will add to our general view of human psycho-dynamics. I believe that it will be determined that all persons, to some extent or another, have multiple selves. We will also come to a better understanding of the nature of healthy ego states as a counter balance to our multiplicity. Finally, I think that we will find ways to take advantage of our multiplicity to accelerate our inherent abilities and talents.

In this regard, I am reminded of a most remarkable client, whom I will call Gerald.

Gerald, a man in his late forties, had been referred to me by his counselor with the approval of his attending physician. It was a late summer afternoon in July when he walked into my office. Two and a half years earlier, Gerald had suffered a devastating and disabling stroke.

By this time in his recovery, he had regained about a third of his previous functioning. According to prevailing medical opin-ion this is about all he could expect.

Gerald limped very slowly into my office with the assistance of a cane and dragging his left foot beside him. His speech was somewhat slurred, and he was easily confused.

I was to have received a copy of his medical records before he arrived, but for some reason they never got to my office. I first had Gerald give me a body scan, telling me what areas of his body he was aware of. Most of his left side was absent from his awareness, an indicator of how massive the damage to his brain had been. He reported to me that he was in almost constant pain.

As part of my assessment, I had Gerald raise his left arm as high as he could. He barely lifted it off his lap, perhaps two or three inches.

It was then that a most amazing thing happened.

I asked Gerald to recall a time when he felt he had been at his physical peak of vitality and strength. He closed his eyes for a moment and said "nineteen," when he had just gotten out of the Army.

I had him return, in his imagination, to that time in his life. As I spoke, I put on some soft music to induce a deeper brain state and suggested to him that the nineteen-year-old of his youth was now somehow inexplicably inside his body. I asked him to allow the nineteen-year-old self to raise his left arm and just allow it to happen.

Almost immediately his arm began to rise from his lap. He had reached up to just over his shoulder before he stopped. I happened to glance over at his wife, who was sitting literally on the edge of her seat, tears streaming down her face.

"He's never been able to do that!" she said.

Looking back at our first meeting, I think my ignorance of Gerald's medical prognosis had actually served us. Without having an expert's opinion about the extent of the damage and what could or could not be expected, I was not hindered by any preconceptions.

Gerald continued to make progress. The pain in his body dissipated, his speech improved and his balance got better. His improvement was so marked that his physical therapists commented on it as did his stroke support group.

A central feature of our work was the memories of his earlier more healthy time. We used this leverage to create change. I cannot substantiate this scientifically since there were no controls in our work. But I feel that whenever Gerald tapped into his nineteen-year-old self while in the deeper brain states, his neurology actually changed in some respect. Given enough time and enough repetition, this temporary healthy neurology positively affected his damaged brain and nervous system.

In similar ways, it is possible for normal persons to tap into the latent power of their own other selves. Athletes, for instance, may tap into their "Super Athlete Self" to give them a competitive edge. Artists and writers may access more masterful selves resulting in more superlative work. The list goes on.

And what if it were possible for you to gain access to your own multiplicity and find healthier, stronger, and more competent or creative selves? What if these more resourceful selves could be brought into your awareness in ways that enhanced the very quality of your life?

There are two basic approaches I would like to take in this area. The first is a technique to identify when other selves are operating and how to communicate with them. The second deals with how to access more resourceful selves, and how to coax them into expression.

The Shadow Person

Often times, I find clients in the throws of an aspect of themselves that seems to be much bigger or stronger than they are. I find, too, that often these same people seem unaware of the "other self" running them.

Jeff was a middle management executive who came to see me due to an intractable problem with procrastination. This problem was so bad it had affected his career.

He agonized over the smallest details of things and often went overtime on projects because of it.

In our work together, we uncovered the root of Jeff's obsession. Jeff's father was a highly critical and perfectionistic man. He did not understand children and had inflicted on his son a debilitating handicap. Jeff's father criticized his son for everything. Jeff grew up feeling that he could do nothing right.

One critical incident occurred when he was four years old. He had drawn a crayon picture of a tree and proudly took it to his father who was sitting in the den. His father looked down at the picture and said to his young son: "Are you stupid or something.... trees are green, not blue." And with one fell swoop he crumpled up Jeff's fledgling attempt at self expression and threw it into the trash can.

As a result of his father's unrelenting criticism, Jeff had become paralyzed whenever he was called upon to express an idea or to act in a decisive manner.

Over the years this aspect of himself took on a life of its own. Whenever Jeff was in a situation that demanded action on his part, this other self would surface. In these moments, Jeff would find himself "compelled" to procrastinate, to put off the task as long as possible.

We were able to remedy the situation with a variation of the technique you are about to learn.

I suggest this technique when you are feeling blocked emotionally, when you have the feeling that you are being compelled by some kind of internal force and/or when you feel as if there is "another person" inside of you. You will also find this exercise helpful when you are trying to motivate yourself into taking some kind of positive action that you are resisting. For instance, you might want to communicate with the self that is resisting the action. And you may also wish to communicate with the self that wants to take the action. Understanding is power. And by understanding the various positive and negative forces in yourself, you will be better equipped to deal with them.

An Exercise in Multiplicity

You will need some blank paper and pen for this exercise. You will be communicating with your "other self" by accessing your non-dominant hemisphere. If you are right- handed, for instance, writing with your left hand will access your non-dominant brain. This is due to the fact that your brain switches sides. The right side of the brain controls the left side of the body, and the left side of the brain controls the right side of the body.

For some reason, not quite known to us, much of our unconscious material seems to be stored in or is related to the non-dominant hemisphere.

1. You first want to lower your brain state to a more receptive pattern. Do Level One Breathing for one full sequence. Play the Creative Imagining tape or some other kind of music you find relaxing at low volume in the background.

2. Keeping yourself in this relaxed state of mind, write out a question to this other self with your dominant hand. (If you are right-handed, use your right hand. If you are left-handed, use your left hand.) You might, for instance, ask the other self what it needs or wants from you.

3. Next, pause and switch hands. With your non-dominant hand, write out the response that first comes to your mind from the other self. Don't think about it. Let the words flow onto the page through your non-dominant hand.

4. Dialogue with the other self in this way — writing your

question with the dominant hand and allowing the other self to answer using your non-dominant hand. Write in this way until you are satisfied that you have enough information about its history, desires, and intentions.

5. Your goal in this is to understand this other self and its needs. It is my experience that most other selves can be incorporated in positive ways so that they get their needs met while we get ours met as well. In a few cases this is not possible, but generally it is.

6. Dialogue with your other self with the idea of getting some kind of contract or agreement. Be sure to keep any agreements you make with other selves. Don't make an agreement if you cannot or do not intend to keep it. Other selves can get very nasty if they are crossed or tricked.

7. When working with a particularly powerful self, I suggest that you keep a journal at hand. Record all of your dialogues with this self and make notes of your dreams. These other selves often appear again and again once they are directly contacted.

8. Enjoy the process of discovery. Bringing a "self" into awareness, and owning it, can be a very powerful and positive experience. Through such a process, we become more connected to ourselves and our sense of wholeness often increases. It is not uncommon for persons to experience these moments as holy or sacred, for indeed the root of our word *holy* means whole. The whole self is sacred, and when we are in the act of re-owning ourselves we are involved in a sacred act.

In closing this section on our multiplicity of selves I would like to mention a very personal story.

When I was in the third grade our family was involved in a

very serious car accident which left my brother with severe brain damage. The doctors agreed that he would be a "vegetable" for the rest of his life. They strongly urged my mother to have him institutionalized. While in the hospital, still recuperating from her injuries, she prayed feverishly day and night for God to give her the strength to prove them wrong.

One night, as she lay in her hospital bed, she felt a hand come over her and she heard a voice, which she took to be God, telling her everything would be all right. From that moment on she became the architect of my brother's destiny. When he finally came home, unable to move or talk, she took over his entire rehabilitation. She taught him all over again how to eat, how to walk, how to talk, and how to care for himself.

In the crisis of that moment, my mother had found a way to tap into the vast multiplicity of herself and find the self that could save her son. Today, my brother lives semi-independently — a far cry from the vegetable the experts would have had him become.

There are thousands of stories of men and women who accomplished incredible feats under the most devastating of circumstances. It seems that tribulations often bring out wonderful and noble aspects in people that otherwise rarely see the light of day.

My hope is that we can *all* find ways to bring out our more noble selves without the need for crises, and that these attributes can become a part of our day-to-day lives.

The exercises in Chapter 12 will allow you to access some of the more resourceful selves within you. As you begin this process of mining for psychological gold you may discover a vein of courage, brilliance, and perhaps even genius you never suspected in yourself.

CHAPTER TWELVE

Power States
for Increasing Performance

"There is no security on this earth; there is only opportunity."
— Douglas MacArthur

In this chapter we will explore methods for increasing your performance and confidence in specific areas. While these include such diverse interests as public speaking, test taking, career and sports, they all share a common element: you will alter your brain state to achieve these goals.

The techniques you will use to do this have been covered in the previous chapters. If you have not read and mastered the exercises in Chapters 4, 5, and 6, please return to them now. You cannot successfully do the techniques in this chapter unless you have mastered the previous exercises.

Look over the protocols on the following pages and go through those that seem to address areas of your interest.

Eliminating Fear of Tests and Exams

Many people suffer from test or exam anxiety and find themselves unable to fully demonstrate their level of knowledge under such situations.

It is important to note that this protocol does not take the place of *studying* for a test, but it will effectively reduce or eliminate anxiety around test taking or exams.

In this exercise, you must be able to "calibrate" yourself. This means that you will be asked to monitor your own relative states of tension and relaxation. If you are not clear how to notice when you are tense or relaxed, please refer to Chapter 8 before going any further.

The steps in this protocol should be done in order and exactly as directed. Read through the entire protocol first, before doing it.

1. Establishing an anchor: If your test is a written test, you will want to get a pencil or pen. College entrance exams such as SATs and many company exams require a number two pencil. Most other school exams are taken in pen. Get hold of a pen or pencil, as needed. We will come back to this later in the protocol. If the test is an oral exam, you need nothing.

2. Imagine yourself in the exam room or location of your test. If you don't actually know what the test area looks like, imagine something sterile or neutral like a bare room. As you imagine receiving and then taking the test, note your level of tension and your breathing. Notice especially the muscles in your forehead, your jaw, your neck, and around your eyes.

3. Now let go of the images and feelings around the imagined exam.

4. Recall a time and a situation where you felt very, very relaxed. Perhaps it was sitting in a big comfortable chair or floating in a warm bath or lying in the sun. Whatever this

situation was, remember it now, and, as you recall this memory, allow yourself to feel the relaxation in your body.

Let the memory of the actual situation go so that you are left with only the pleasant and relaxing feelings in your body. Intensify these pleasant and relaxing feelings. Notice your decreased level of tension. Notice the level of relaxation in your forehead, your jaw, your neck, and around your eyes.

If the level of tension is not markedly decreased from when you imagined taking the test or exam in Step 2, you have not, as yet, built in this resource of relaxation strong enough to be effective. Go back through Step 4 until you very clearly and strongly feel these sensations of relaxation in your body. You may wish to go through the Two Minute Stress Buster a couple of times, followed by Level One Breathing before recalling the relaxing situation.

5. Run through the sequence in Step 4 several times until you can recreate these feelings of relaxation almost instantly and at will just by thinking about them.
6. If your exam is oral, you will need to create an anchor to "fire off" these feelings of relaxation and confidence yourself without being noticed. This is actually quite easy to do. You can, for instance, lightly touch your forefinger to your thumb or touch yourself in any manner such as placing your hands in your lap. The important thing to do is to decide on the anchor that you will use and to use it consistently.

If your exam is written, I suggest that you use a pen or pencil as your anchor.
Note: The GRE is being converted to a computer format over the next several years. For such exams, you will need to use a "mouse" as your anchor.

7. Recreate the feelings of relaxation you developed in Step 4, and when you are experiencing them at their strongest point (in other words, when you are most relaxed) "fire off" the anchor. If you are using a touch for your anchor (for example your forefinger to your thumb), hold this gesture while you feel the strong feelings of relaxation. If you are using a pen or pencil, hold it in your writing hand between the fingers you use to write while you experience the relaxing feelings. Hold the anchor for about five to ten seconds while you recall the feelings of relaxation. Release the anchor and bring yourself back to a neutral feeling — not feeling anything in particular.

8. Repeat Step 7 three or four times. In other words, recreate the feelings of relaxation and then "fire off" the anchor as you feel those relaxing feelings for about five to ten seconds. The most important points are to 1) hold the relaxing feeling at its strongest level when and while you "fire off" the anchor and 2) hold the pen or pencil or touch yourself in exactly the same way each time — same place, same pressure, etc.

In the above steps you have stimulated your brain to associate an anchor with the feeling of relaxation, which is the opposite of anxiety. In the next steps, we will test to make sure that your brain has linked these together: anchor and relaxation.

9. Sit and hold your mind in a neutral place; have no particular thought or feeling. Without changing your thought or feeling in any way, "fire off" the anchor and see if it makes you feel more relaxed. If it tends to bring you back to the feeling of relaxation, no matter how light, your brain has successfully linked the anchor and resource state (relaxation) together. Now all you need do is reinforce the association. Go through this step again and again, "firing

off" the anchor and intensifying the feeling. Go through this sequence several times until just "firing off" the anchor brings you instantly and deeply into relaxation. If "firing off" the anchor does not bring back feelings of relaxation go back through Steps 4 through 8.

10. Go back to Step 2 and imagine yourself taking the test or exam and re-calibrate yourself to notice where and how much tension you have at the idea of taking the test.

11. Imagine yourself taking the exam, and as you do "fire off" and hold the anchor until you feel relaxed. Go through this step over and over until "firing off" the anchor instantly re-creates feelings of relaxation, even in the midst of imagining yourself taking the test or exam.

Now that you have successfully linked the resource state of relaxation to your anchor while under a stressful situation (taking the test or exam), you are ready to "future pace" your brain into that reality. Through the process of future pacing you can greatly increase the power of your anchor.

12. **Future Pacing**: Imagine yourself taking the test or exam and when you get a sense of this fantasy, imagine "firing off" the anchor. Don't actually fire off the anchor, just imagine yourself doing it. Notice how the feelings of relaxation reduce or eliminate any tension or anxiety you may have felt.

If this future pacing does not re-create the resource state of relaxation, it is not yet fully anchored into your nervous system. If this is the case, simply go back over steps 7 through 11.

You have now anchored in a powerful resource state that guarantees the reduction or elimination of anxiety in test taking because it is neurologically impossible for you to feel relaxed *and* anxious at the same time.

By practicing this protocol several times, you will be able to eliminate anxiety around test taking.

Eliminating Fear of Public Speaking

If you are someone who is afraid of speaking in public, you know how debilitating this phobia can be. For some it is just an annoying problem, while for others it can damage self-esteem and hold back career advancement.

Regardless of why this fear started, it is basically created out of how you organize your internal maps or representations. In the protocol below, you will alter your internal perception and introduce new resources. This combination will greatly reduce or eliminate your fear around speaking in public.

Read through the entire exercise first and then go through it as directed.

1. **Calibrating your level of fear:** Imagine yourself in front of a large group of people (or a small group if this is what creates fear in you). As you imagine yourself talking in front of this group of people note your level of tension and your breathing. Especially pay attention to the muscles in your forehead, your jaw, your neck, and around your eyes. Note this level of tension for future reference.

2. Now let go of the images and feelings around this imagined situation.

3. Recall a time and a situation in which you felt very, very relaxed. Perhaps it was while floating in a warm bath, lying in the warm sun, or sitting comfortably in a big chair. Remember this situation now, whatever it was, and, as you recall this memory, allow yourself to feel those feelings of relaxation in your body. Let the memory of the actual situation go, so that you are left with pleasant and relaxing feelings in your body. Intensify these pleasant and relaxing feelings. Notice your decreased level of tension. Notice the level of relaxation in your forehead, your

jaw, your neck, and around the eyes. If the level of tension is not markedly decreased from when you imagined speaking in front of a group in Step 1, you have not yet built in this resource of relaxation strong enough to be effective. Go back through Step 3 until you clearly and strongly feel these sensations of relaxation in your body.

4. Run through the sequence in Step 3 several times until you can recreate these feelings of relaxation almost instantly and at will just by thinking about it.

5. **Establishing an anchor:** We are now going to program into your brain this resource state of relaxation. For this purpose we will use the anchor of gently touching the left or right forefinger to its corresponding thumb. This is the suggested anchor, but you can use any other anchor you feel would work for you in front of a group of people.

6. **Testing the anchor:** Recreate the feelings of relaxation you created in step 3, and when you are experiencing them at their strongest point (in other words, when you are most relaxed) "fire off" the anchor. Hold the anchor for about five to ten seconds as you experience the feelings of relaxation. Then release the anchor and bring yourself back to a neutral feeling — not feeling anything in particular.

7. Repeat Step 6 three or four times. In other words, recreate the feelings of relaxation and then "fire off" the anchor as you feel those relaxing feelings for about five to ten seconds. The most important points are to 1) hold the relaxing feeling at its strongest level when and while you "fire off" the anchor and 2) hold the anchor in exactly the same way each time — same place, same pressure, etc.

8. Hold your mind in a neutral place with no particular thought or feeling. Without changing your thought or feeling in any way, "fire off" the anchor and see if it makes you feel more relaxed. If it tends to bring you back to the

feeling of relaxation, no matter how light, your brain has successfully linked the anchor and resource state (relaxation) together. Now you need to reinforce the association. Go through this step again and again, "firing off" the anchor and intensifying the feeling, becoming more and more relaxed with each firing of the anchor. Go through this sequence several times until just "firing off" the anchor brings you instantly and deeply into relaxation. If "firing off" the anchor does not bring back feelings of relaxation, go back over Steps 3 through 7.

9. Next, imagine that you are watching yourself giving a talk. Fire off your relaxation anchor by touching your thumb and forefinger. Simply watch yourself in this imaginary situation as you experience this relaxed state of awareness. In other words, you are relaxed and unconcerned as you watch yourself giving a presentation. Make sure that you are feeling relaxed as you imagine watching yourself give this talk. If you are not feeling relaxed, go back to Steps 6 through 7.

10. In this next step, we will "associate" you with the image of yourself. Still holding the anchor, imagine that you are now inside your imaginary body giving this imaginary presentation. Allow yourself to experience yourself giving a talk confidently and in a relaxed manner. Notice how you are holding and moving your body. Imagine, in detail, how you feel and move in this imaginary, relaxed, and confident body. If you find yourself getting "up tight" as you imagine yourself in this way, you have not built in the resources of relaxation strongly enough. If this is the case, return to Step 3.

11. You are now ready to "neuromuscularly program" your newfound confidence around public speaking. Get your body into the posture of your "imaginary body" in Step 10. Stand or sit in this way. As you physically move your

body, re-enacting your presentation as much as possible, remember the relaxed feelings you generated earlier. If you need to, you can "fire off" the anchor for relaxation as needed. Take several minutes to experience yourself being relaxed in the physical postures you will take during your presentation. Be sure to include sitting, standing, and walking postures to cover as many situations as possible.

12. Finally, you will want to Future Pace these new resources of relaxation and confidence around public speaking. Imagine yourself giving a talk, perhaps a specific talk if one is on your schedule. Watch yourself both from the dissociated and associated positions. In other words, start off observing yourself as if from the outside, watching how you stand, move, and talk. Then, as you recognize that you are relaxed, associate with the image and allow yourself to experience how you feel both physically and emotionally with these new resources of relaxation and confidence.

If you have a strong phobic reaction to public speaking, it would be best for you to go over the above protocol on a regular basis (two or more times a week) until you distinctly feel a growing sense of confidence. You may also wish to use the protocol on alternate selves (Chapter 11) to uncover self-sabotage elements.

Powering up to Be Your Best

The following technique can be used whenever you need to be your best: public speaking, sports competition, artistic performance. The list is endless. Wherever or whenever you find yourself in a situation that demands more than you seem to have, this exercise can be a life saver.

I have used it, myself, on various occasions. One incident stands out particularly. My wife and I were in Hong Kong conducting a series of performance seminars for corporations in the hotel and training industries. Our itinerary required me to do a major presentation to a group of senior executives several hours after our arrival from the United States. The plane trip had taken twenty-four hours, and I was suffering from extreme jet lag.

I was not in the best of states to give such an important presentation, but I had no choice in the matter. I could struggle through the talk and wish for the best, or I could access another more resourceful part of me. This part was not jet lagged, exhausted, or in an ill mood. It was quite relaxed, alert, and eager to share the information on human performance that I had come to present.

This other self was constructed on the spot using aspects of the technique you are about to learn. While in this "other self," I experienced a whole new level of energy. The seminar went flawlessly, and there was tremendous interest in the work after I had finished. Once the task was complete, I returned to the hotel and caught up on some much needed sleep!

This protocol below will help you to access your own inner resourceful self and, as I said earlier, it can be effectively used in a number of different situations.

Please read over the entire exercise before going through it.

Accessing a Resourceful Self
1. Determine the mental, emotional, and physical state you wish to access. For instance, in my Hong Kong presentation mentioned earlier, my mental state needed to be one of clarity. The emotional state needed to be poised and confident. The required physical state was one of energy.
2. Recall a time when you experienced these mental, emotional, and physical states. If there was not a time when you experienced all of these states together, then recall each state, one at a time. For instance, if you wish to access the states I used in my Hong Kong presentation, you would remember experiencing clarity sometime in the

past. Let yourself feel this clarity as you remember it. Then move on to remembering a time when you felt poised and confident. Let yourself feel this emotional state and then add the previous mental clarity so that you are experiencing both of them together. Then let yourself feel the sensation of having physical energy. Now put all three states together so that you are feeling clear, poised, confidence, and energetic.

Note: If you have never actually experienced any or all of these states in your past, this is not a problem. Simply create a fantasy in which you imagine experiencing these states. Imagine what they would feel like. If you allow yourself to imagine these resourceful states in detail, they will have a similar effect on the nervous system as if you remembered them. This is because the unconscious mind does not know the difference between a real and an imagined event.

3. Next, you need to lower your brain state using Level One Breathing.

4. Now have a brief fantasy of yourself actually doing the task you wish to accomplish with the mental, emotional, and physical states that you have to set up. In the case of my Hong Kong presentation, I had a fantasy in which I was vibrantly full of energy and confident, poised, and clear about my subject.

Experience yourself being incredibly successful at the task. When you have a strong sense of this, move your awareness into your "fantasy body," the one with the resourceful states in your imagination. Experience this fantasy as if it were real. Use your senses. See yourself, hear the sounds, feel the physical sensations and emotions. Make it as real as you can. Try especially to get the kinesthetic (felt) sense of what it is like to be in that fantasy body.

5. Next, take a moment to move your actual physical body into the postures and ways of moving and holding yourself that you experienced in your fantasy. This neuromuscularly programs the associations, making them much stronger in the brain.
6. To access this self in the near future, all you need do is to move your body into the holding or moving pattern of your fantasy body and recall the mental, emotional, and physical states you have programmed. Some people deepen their sense of being in the resourceful self by adding a short word or phrase that they say to themselves such as: "Yes!," "You can do it," or "Go for it."

Ideally you should go through this exercise several times before you do the actual task, at which time you simply move your body into the associated posture to access your "resourceful self."

There are other ways to access other more resourceful selves as well. But I have found the combination of positive fantasy and bodily (kinesthetic) programming to be a very potent combination.

Improving Sports Performance

A unique study with basketball players revealed a rather interesting facet of what is now being called "Inner Training."

Four groups of players were selected and evaluated on their free throwing abilities. One group did nothing in terms of practicing. Another group practiced in the usual manner, actually shooting free throws. A third group practiced in their minds. That is, they actually didn't practice at all, but went through the steps of free throwing in their imagination. A fourth group both practiced in the usual manner and in their minds.

As expected, the group which did nothing showed the least improvement. But surprisingly, the group practiced only in their minds scored close to the group which physically practiced free throwing. The fourth group, the ones who practiced with their minds and with their bodies, showed the greatest improvement.

Other studies and anecdotal reports from sports psychologists have upheld the implications this study. It seems that a combination of mental training in conjunction with actual physical conditioning gives athletes a cutting edge.

In the following protocol, you will learn how to mentally train yourself for any sport, thereby increasing your level of performance.

One of the crucial elements in this kind of training is what I call "kinesthetic detail." Kinesthetic awareness is what allows a tennis player, for example, to know where his or her racket hand is even though he or she may not actually be looking at it. Kinesthetic detail is what tells the player if the racket is in the proper position or not, i.e. the angle required to hit the ball where he or she wants it to go. All expert players, without exception, have a highly developed sense of kinesthetic detail.

Each sport has its own unique set of movements, thus the kinesthetic detail required for tennis is different from that required for golf or swimming.

It is important that you consciously identify the kinesthetic details required in your sport before you practice the following protocol. The reason for this caution has to do with the power of this exercise. Whatever you program into your brain with this protocol will be coded into the neuromuscular patterning part of your brain. And once it is set, it will be difficult to change it, although it can be done. My advice is that if you are not sure of the fine detailed movements required in your sport, get hold of a good coach or trainer to walk you through them — before you program your brain.

Inner Training Protocol

Before going through this exercise, consciously determine those movements you want to program into your brain. The goal is for you to do these movements, without having to think about them, whenever you are playing your chosen sport.

For most sports, you will need to break the skills down into several different categories. In tennis, for instance, the movements for a backhand or a forehand are different. In golf, the movements in making a putt are quite different from teeing off.

After you have familiarized yourself with the actual physical movements required for a certain skill, you are ready for the exercise.

Read through the protocol first and then go through it as described.

1. Play the Creative Imagining tape or other music that you find relaxing and which helps you turn your attention "inward."

2. Do Level One Breathing.

3. After completing Level One Breathing, allow yourself to breathe in long, slow, comfortable inhales and long, slow, comfortable exhales. Breathe in this way as you go through the entire exercise.

4. Imagine that you can sense an image of yourself going through the correct movements as if you are having a waking dream and can watch a movie of yourself. Watch yourself going through the perfect moves. (Note: It is not necessary to actually see yourself. A felt sense of yourself is fine.)

5. As you continue to breathe long, slow, and comfortably, shift your awareness back from being aware of watching yourself to being aware of going through the movements. For this second step, you will use something called your "imaginary kinesthetic body." You want to get the feel of what it is like to physically move your body through these correct movements. A swimmer practicing his butterfly stroke might get a sense of watching himself from the side of the pool or from a vantage point of underneath himself.

Making sure that he is doing the moves correctly, he then imagines himself actually going through the movements in his mind. He imagines feeling the pressure of the water against his arms, the sound of the water coming up over his ears, and the arch of his back. He feels all of the various details required for the actual movement. This kinesthetic or bodily feeling of detail is crucial. It is through this imaginary movement that he is neuromuscularly programming his brain.

6. Take two to five minutes to go through this process of watching yourself and then feeling yourself go through the correct movements.

The next time you actually play your sport, focus on the feel of the movements. Notice how closely they match the movements you have been programming.

After your practice session, go back through the protocol again, preferably within twenty-four hours. This process of both imagining the movements and actually making them will "lock" them into the movement patterning areas of your brain. They will become automatic, allowing you to become aware of even finer kinesthetic detail.

The ideal way to use this protocol is in tandem with physical training. After every training session go through the protocol. Use the Physical Training/Inner Training Cycle until you are satisfied with your performance.

Recuperating from Sports Injuries

Sports injuries are especially difficult, both for attending physicians and athletes.

These types of injuries are difficult for physicians because athletes are prone to re-enter sports activity before recovery is complete. This often results in further injury, making the physician's work more difficult.

Many athletes confronted with not being able to get their usual "high" from working out become depressed and uncooperative.

In such cases, Inner Training can be very beneficial. If athletes recuperating from an injury practice the Inner Training Protocol on a regular basis, it should help them stick with the recuperation program set up by their physician. When these athletes finally re-enter their sport, they will be amazed at how well they perform.

I also suggest that they practice the Thymic Breathing Exercise (Chapter 9). These two, Inner Training and Thymic Breathing should be practiced every day until the attending physician says that it is o.k. to begin the sport again.

CHAPTER THIRTEEN

The Acoustic Brain: Changing Brain State Through Sound

"The world is sound."

— *Nada Brahma*

I t would seem that to be human is to be deeply responsive to music. Most cultures create some kind of music and many have raised it to an art form. Music can speak to our deepest emotions, and it can speak to our neurophysiology as well.

In a study at a New York City hospital, Sue Chapman, M.D., played Brahms to a group of premature infants. These "Brahms Babies" listened to the stringed version of the Brahms Lullaby several times a day. This was the only difference between their treatment and the control group, which did not listen to music. The result was both interesting and challenging to our traditional models of medicine.

The Brahms Babies had fewer complications, gained weight

faster, and were released from the hospital an average of a week earlier than the control group.

How did the playing of music have such a profound effect upon the physical health of these infants?

From the standpoint of psychoacoustics it is very clear what happened. Psychoacoustics is the study of how sound, language, and music affect the human nervous system and behavior. And to understand the effects of the Brahms Lullaby, we must look at the brain.

The auditory pathways enter the brain through the medulla oblongata (first level) and are enervated into a structure called the Reticular Activating System or RAS. The RAS is responsible for alerting or sedating the neocortex in relationship to incoming sensory information. The RAS is also diffused throughout much of the brain and can thereby affect other structures and areas.

The calm rhythms and soothing timbre of the Brahms Lullaby were, as a result, diffused throughout the growing brains of these tiny vulnerable infants. This presumably reduced the levels of stress hormones, lowered respiration and heart rate, and allowed the process of development to take place under less duress.

Although the classical composers did not have access to highly sophisticated research equipment, many of them clearly appreciated the abilities of music to alter awareness.

Johannes Sebastian Bach had a friend named Count Kayserling, a Russian envoy, who suffered from bouts of insomnia. It seems the count asked Bach to write something that could be played at night to help him to go to sleep. Bach wrote a series of short pieces and named them after Kayserling's personal harpsichordist, a man named Goldberg. Evidently, the Goldberg Variations were successful, and story has it that Kayserling slept like a baby.

When Dr. Lozanov of the Lozanov Institute in Bulgaria

conducted EEG studies of persons listening to the Goldberg Variations, he discovered something of interest. The Variations created an increase of Alpha activity, a known precursor to the slower brain activity of sleep.

Lozanov discovered, through his EEG studies, that there was a whole class of music from the Baroque period that increased Alpha activity in listeners. These "largo" movements were played at a rhythm of sixty beats per minute. He noted that music at this rhythm increased Alpha activity by an average of six percent while decreasing Beta activity in the neighborhood of six percent.

In other words, just listening to this music changes brain state. The listener begins to feel more relaxed and calm. Pulse slows by an average of four divisions of mercury, respiration slows down, and subjects report a "relaxed awareness."

Later in his studies, Dr. Lozanov discovered that he could greatly accelerate learning by using this kind of music. His method has become known in the United States as Superlearning or the Lozanov method, and it is a very effective method for accelerating learning, especially of rote materials such as foreign languages.

We know from numerous studies that sound and music can affect the processing of information in our neocortex, the area of the brain responsible for thought. But sound and music can also profoundly affect the emotional circuitry of our brains.

Many years ago Alfred Tomatis, M.D., a French physician, was called to a Benedictine Monastery outside Paris, where most of the monks had become severely depressed, listless, and uninterested in eating. Upon investigation of the circumstances surrounding the sudden outbreak of the communal depression, Tomatis discovered that the monastery had recently acquired a new Abbot.

The new head of the monastery thought of himself as a

modern man and considered Gregorian chanting to be too "medieval." He therefore stopped all chanting shortly after his arrival. Unfortunately chanting was about the only form of auditory stimulation the monks received.

When Tomatis had the Abbot reinstate the chanting, the monks' depression miraculously lifted. This led Tomatis to investigate how certain frequency ranges affect the brain. His work led him to explore the high range frequencies, and it resulted in a technique known as the Tomatis Method of sound healing.

In the Tomatis Method, a special form of audiogram, called an "Electronic Ear," is used to detect deficient frequency ranges in the subject.

The subject then listens to music that is filtered to enhance those frequency ranges in which he or she is deficient. This evidently retrains the ear to hear those frequencies it deleted for whatever reason. Somehow the reintegration of these previously missing frequencies stimulates the brain into new states of awareness and capabilities. It is often effective with certain types of learning disabilities as well as emotional problems.

One of the interesting psychological benefits of this method is that as subjects begin to retrain their ears, they often re-experience the trauma or shock that caused them to delete the specific range of frequencies.

It could have been, for instance, that an abusive parent yelled at a subject when he or she was a child. For argument's sake let's say this parent bellowed the verbal abuse in the 1200Hz range.

The child might have literally deleted this frequency from his or her own hearing for protection. If, for examples, this frequency is needed for the brain to perceive certain types of patterns such as language or math, the person will have difficulty in these areas. Years later, through sound therapy such as the Tomatis method, the adult may actually re-experience episodes of his or her childhood that caused the original deletion to occur.

With the advent of modern research methods, science is now documenting the powerful effects of sound on brain physiology and behavior. But sound has been used as a means to affect health and to alter awareness for thousands of years.

Shamans from indigenous cultures throughout the world have used and continue to use chanting and drumming as a means to heal and to enter the "dream world" of consciousness.

In a study of shamanic drumming, Melinda Maxfield, Ph.D., documented that such drumming "has specific neurophysi-ological effects and the ability to elicit temporary changes in brain wave activity." Such drumming is known to facilitate certain kinds of mental imagery and alterations of awareness. Such alterations of consciousness would, presumably, be depen-dent upon alterations of brain wave activity. Specifically, Dr. Maxfield documented that drumming patterns of around four to four and a half beats per second tend to generate an increase in Theta activity.

The records of many ancient cultures reveal a highly sophis-ticated understanding about the relationships between sound and human consciousness, even though they lacked modern scientific research facilities.

One pre-historical society is of special interest in this regard. Vedic India possessed a rich and sophisticated culture hundreds of years before Christ. The Vedic Rishis, or seers, developed highly advanced methods of inner-exploration and had, as a result, intuited the structure of consciousness itself. To this day, the Vedas offer one of the most intriguing and detailed maps of human consciousness.

Out of their discoveries, a tradition of mantra and yantra developed, which has been handed down from generation to generation.

A mantra is a sound such as the Tibetan mantra "Om mani padme om" or the Christian mantra "Amen."

In the Vedic tradition all mantras have a corresponding visual representation called a yantra. And supposedly, in this tradition, an initiate (one who has been trained in these teachings) can hear a mantra and "see" its yantra in his or her mind's eye. It is also possible for such an initiate to see a yantra and "hear" in his or her mind the corresponding mantra. The two, mantra and yantra, are interchangeable.

Researchers in Cymatics, a science that studies the effects of sound vibration, have verified the essential truth about mantra and yantra as laid down by the ancient Rishis.

Using a special electronic device called a tonoscope, it is possible to get the visual image or geometric pattern of any sound. When the mantra "om" is uttered correctly, it makes a geometric pattern remarkably similar to the ancient Shri Yantra for "om."

It would seem that science is verifying that the ancient sages had, in fact, intuited the very structure of sound. If this is true, how did they do it?

Before we address this intriguing question, consider the following riddle.

Chopin, a noted classical composer, wrote a piece called the Funeral March in the seventeenth century.

Some three hundred years later in a modern DNA research facility, a geneticist by the name of Susumu Ohno, D.V.M., Ph.D., D.SC. ascribed musical notation to the building blocks of DNA. Using computer technology, Dr. Ohno printed out the musical notation for the beginning DNA sequences of genes and found that they were not random noise, but recognizable melodies. While working with the gene for a kind of cancer, Dr. Ohno recognized the basic melody. It was from Chopin's Funeral March.

Questions concerning human intuition such as exhibited by Chopin and the ancient Rishis cannot, at present, be answered through the scientific method. But they do pose some fascinating challenges to our limited ways of logical thinking and perceiving.

If it is true, as quantum physics suggests, that we are part and parcel of a great and vibrating universe, and if it is true that our brains, and thus our minds, are created from swirls and vortexes of subatomic forces, would it not be possible for "the mind" to contact or intuit some of its own underpinnings?

Dr. Ohno's work would seem to corroborate some ancient ideas and concepts in health. The phrase "in harmony" is often used to denote a sense of well-being, while "out of harmony" is sometimes used to denote a sense of disease.

If Dr. Ohno's ideas are accurate, and I personally believe they are, each of the organs in our bodies is "singing" its own melody. Health is when our organs and systems are "singing" in harmony, and disease is when they are in dissonance or in conflict.

If we had ears to hear the full range of vibrational frequencies, we might hear ourselves as walking symphonies. This may be one reason why certain types of music appeal to different people. It may go beyond mere taste and level of sophistication. It could be that the musical patterns in a piece of music may enhance or conflict with a person's own inherent musical pattern. And indeed, in studies on music and healing, one of the most important elements observed was that the subject had to like the music.

One of the essential elements in music is something rarely discussed because there is no real vocabulary to describe it, and at present there is no way to measure or quantify it, which takes it immediately out of the range of science. Still, nevertheless, I feel compelled to discuss it.

This essential element is consciousness. Consciousness is

what enlivens sound into information, be it the toning of a shaman or the breath-taking movement of a symphony.

Sound as information is created via the agency of consciousness itself. A mother reading a book while her infant plays in the next room may not give much thought to the babbling and cooing of her child. But should the infant become truly distressed, the mother would instantly know from the sound of the child's voice. And although the child cannot speak with words, it speaks with an ancient and primordial voice that commands instant attention.

Manfred Clynes, the noted musician and researcher from Australia, has studied sound patterning for many years. Using a special device, he has documented that human emotion has distinct wave forms and that it is possible to convey emotion purely through sound wave forms without the need for language at all. He calls these wave forms "essentic waves," and he has documented that universal human emotions have the same essentic wave form characteristics no matter what culture they are from. In other words, love has the same wave form in Japan as it does in Libya as it does in New York.

What is it then that differentiates the musical performance of a master like a Segovia or a Horowitz, an Eric Clapton or a Jimmy Hendrix from other talented musicians? It is a combination of talent and training, yes. But it is also something else. It is how the musician brings himself or herself to bear through the music. This process of expressing one's identity or passion through sound patterning whether it be a concerto for violin or an electric guitar in a rock band is essentially the same. The mediums are merely different.

A truly great performer is able to enliven the music through the sheer intention of his or her consciousness. And I believe such a performer intuitively expresses into the music essentic forms of human emotion and desire. Such wave forms cannot be captured on a sheet of music. They emerge from the spirit or consciousness of the performer.

Spaces Between the Music

There is another element crucial to music. And it is so obvious, it would be easy to overlook. But without it, there could be no music nor anything else for that matter. This element is silence or space.

Take this book for instance. If there were not space, there would be no way to differentiate it from anything else around you. It would all be one big blob. Space is crucial to meaning.

The patterning of sound into music also requires a type of space. When a phrase ends in a piece of music, we recognize it because there is a pause, a silence or space.

In the esoteric, or hidden traditions of Buddhism, there is a sense that all things emerge out of an essential nothingness or space. And quantum physics would seem to bear out this view of things.

The direct experience of the space or nothingness in which we move and have our being can be rather disturbing for some, but it has tremendous benefits.

The following exercise is a Tibetan Sound Meditation that brings you into a direct awareness of the space or silence from which all sound vibration emerges.

It develops subtle perception and intuition and has a very calming influence on the body and mind.

Tibetan Sound Meditation

1. Sit in a comfortable position and close your eyes.
2. Let your breath be slow and calm, taking about six seconds for the inhale and about six seconds for the exhale. Breathe

in this way for a minute or so before going on to Step 3.

3. Continuing to breathe in this calm and slow pattern, move your awareness into the sounds around you. But instead of focusing your attention on the sounds themselves, focus on the space or silence around the sound.

4. Get a sense of the spatial orientation of each sound. That is, notice if a particular sound is close or faraway, above you or below you, etc.

5. Try to get a felt sense of the space or silence around each sound you hear and of the greater space that holds all of the sounds including you. Practice this form for ten to thirty minutes, longer if you wish.

Practicing this meditation once a day for thirty days or so will generate profound benefits, including a greater sense of calm and peace as well as health benefits associated with reduced stress. In addition, the consistent practice of this meditation will give you a deep and intuitive knowledge of how sound and vibration relate to your own consciousness.

By practicing this meditation form, you will eventually reach profound states of altered consciousness. You may experience yourself as a field of energy, as a point of consciousness hovering in space, or in a deep and abiding sense of calm. This meditation reveals to you the essential "nothingness" of creation out of which the universe emerges. It is a powerful process, but one has to experience it for one's self to appreciate it.

(A Note on Mindfulness: This meditation requires you to consistently keep your focus on your sense of space and silence. Your mind will probably wander from attending to the space/silence and into thoughts. That is simply what "the mind" does. When you become aware that you have wandered off into thought or fantasy, just gently bring your attention back to the space/silence. Don't judge yourself for going off into thought, just bring yourself back to a mindfulness of the space/silence. Most people "go off" several times in the course of a sitting.)

The metaphors of the gods have been replaced for many by quarks and bosons and other subatomic particles. The body of quantum physics, though secular, would agree with both Genesis and the Vedas. The universe was set into existence through vibration. The universe, itself, is vibration.

Everything in physical existence, from the giant pulsars of the night sky to the book you hold in your hands to your hands themselves, are in vibration. We can't sense this vibration, for the most part, because we are a part of it. It is like trying to separate the waft from the weave in a tapestry. It cannot be done without losing the design.

The illusion of solidity is a magic trick of the atomic world. To use a metaphor from atomic physics, the electrons in the outer shells of atoms spin at such fantastic speeds, they create the mirage of solidness to our nervous systems.

Take an old airplane propeller. Sitting still you can easily see that it consists of two or three props, but when the engine begins to spin them, they appear as a solid disk. Thus it is with all seemingly solid objects. Material objects are mostly space.

In fact, it has been estimated that if you took away the space within your body, you would be able to fit all of the matter that actually comprises your body onto the tip of a pin.

We are immersed in space, and our very nature is emptiness. In order, then, to truly understand vibration and sound as well as the pulsation of consciousness itself, we must understand emptiness.

In modern Western cultures, emptiness is almost taboo. People are phobic about it. We dare not stop for a moment lest we become aware of the essential emptiness of things. But it is in this emptiness that much healing awaits us. Emptiness is not the same as annihilation.

Emptiness is a crack in the egg of our perception. Through it we can enter a different kind of reality, one which is more fluid and less limited than our day-to-day time-bound reality.

The alternate states of awareness that you can create for yourself using the methods in this book allow you to pass through this crack in perception.

Drumming and Toning

In the previous chapters, we discussed how you could change your brain state by such devices as changing your breathing and by altering your mental experience.

In this chapter, I want to show you how you can make use of humankind's most ancient of methods for altering consciousness. It dates back thousands of years before Christ, even before civilization as we know it.

In almost all indigenous cultures on earth, toning, the making of sound through the human voice, and drumming are essential parts of healing.

Analysis of the drumming patterns from different shamanic cultures reveals a vast complexity of rhythm. As mentioned earlier, these rhythms have the ability to "entrain" the brain into altered states of awareness. Entrainment is a term in psychoacoustics that refers to the effects of a repetitive sound pattern on brain wave patterning.

Very simplistically, a fast sound pattern tends to speed up brain wave activity while a slow sound pattern will slow down brain wave activity.

By playing a repetitive drum rhythm over and over, a shaman or most anyone, for that matter, can induce an altered state of awareness. This is accomplished by the shaman using his or her intuitive abilities, but modern psychoacoustics has mapped out the effects of entrainment with mathematical accuracy.

With the advent of electronic tone generators it has become possible to create repetitive sound patterns that can be measured and their effects on the brain documented.

It has been found that if you pulse a tone at 4Hz or four cycles per second, brain activity will tend to move towards that window of entrainment, the threshold between Theta and Delta. If you pulse the same tone at 10Hz, the brain will tend to entrain itself more to the Alpha range of activity. In other words, there will tend to be a statistical increase in Alpha activity.

It is now possible to be a kind of electronic shaman, creating tonal patterns that entrain the brain towards windows of brain wave activity. These windows of brain activity are, in turn, associated with certain types of mental and emotional experiences. (For a more complete discussion of this, review Chapter 4 on brain states.)

This method of altering awareness is being extensively explored by a growing number of psychoacoustic engineers and in the making of psychoacoustic tapes. Such tapes offer a convenient and portable method for altering consciousness. (For a brief discussion of Psychoacoustic tapes developed by the author, please refer to Appendix B.)

Another shamanic sound healing tool is the art of toning.

There are two classes of toning. The first class is used by shamans to alter their own or another's consciousness. The second class of toning is used to heal others.

For our purposes, we will focus on the use of toning to alter one's own consciousness.

An ancient form of toning called Overtone Chanting has some remarkable effects, notably the quick alteration of brain wave patterning and an increase in certain brain chemicals such as endorphins, which are associated with pleasure.

In this method, a vowel sound is toned in such a way as to vibrate the sinuses. Looking at the diagram below, you can see that the hypothalamus and pituitary gland sit near this network of nasal passages. In Overtone Chanting, the sinuses are vibrated and the hypothalamus/pituitary are "massaged" due to the vibrational effect on the sinuses. These two structures create a wide range of brain chemicals including hormones and the morphine-like substance, interphone.

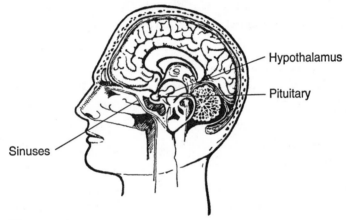

Hypothalamus

Pituitary

Sinuses

Figure 12

I have taught this method to hundreds of people and, although rather esoteric, it is quite easy to learn.

First of all you have to forget any ideas about pretty voices. I have found, over the years, that persons who have the most difficulty with this technique are those who have had formal voice training because, Overtone Chanting goes against everything one learns in classical voice classes. The goal is not to produce beautiful tones, but rather the idea is to vibrate the sinuses. And this is done through nasal tones.

Some people find that if they cup a hand to one of their ears, they can more easily hear the overtones.

Let's start off with the vowel sound "a" (as in ay). Sing this vowel sound. Any pitch will do, but generally the higher pitches work better.

Next, "scrunch" up your nose and make the same "a" sound. You will notice that when you make the sound in this way, it has a nasal quality.

Now go through these vowel sounds, making them nasal as with the "a" sound:

1. Make the "e" vowel sound
2. Make the "i" vowel sound
3. Make the "o" (oh) vowel sound
4. Make the "oo" vowel sound

Next, pretend that you are an infant just learning how to talk. Babies are constantly playing with sound. It is through this process of playing with word "bits" that they are able to make the neurological connections which eventually allow them to make language.

Now, take a deep breath and play with "scrunching" up your nose and slide into making all of the vowel sounds on one breath, slurring the vowels into each other.

Again take a deep breath and get a sense of your sinuses and the areas of your brain that sit on top of them. Make all of the nasal vowel sounds on one breath and sense where the vibration is in these areas of the brain.

Finally, play with making these sounds for a few minutes. Really get a sense of how these sounds stimulate different areas of your brain in relation to the sinuses.

After you have played with the sounds for several minutes notice how you feel, especially in your head. You may notice tingling sensations, or you may sense energy moving or in some cases you may even "see" objects or colors in your mind's eye.

Don't be surprised if you feel giddy or feel like laughing. This technique can release large amounts of endorphins into the blood stream, which is one of the keys to its ability to alter brain state.

If practiced regularly, this method will give parts of your brain a "tune up" through the use of self-generated sound. When used with specific mantras this technique can produce truly profound altered states of awareness. (I have purposely left out these mantras since the premature use of them can unleash difficult to control energy flows in the central nervous system. I would refer the curious reader to a competent Tibetan Tantric Yoga Master for training in this methodology.)

Of all the methods for altering brain state, the use of sound is the most ancient and primordial. Vibration is the fundamental basis of everything that exists, from the stars and galaxies to our bodies and minds.

Our inner ears allow us to hear sound vibration with all of its richness and power, a power that can move us emotionally and heal us physically.

The inner ear is laid out along a spiral very much like the spiral of a nautilus swimming through the ocean or a spiral galaxy floating through space. And although we walk on earth, this is, we now know, only one perspective. From another perspective, just as real, we are moving through a vast sea of vibration. We float through an ocean that is filled to the brim with matter and energy. And this sea, this ocean we live in, is mostly vast space — the same space that galaxies ride into the starry night.

Because our bodies and minds are birthed from this frothy sea, it is possible (should I say probable?) to touch the very substratum of the cosmos by touching the deepest levels of our own awareness. These levels of self-awareness emerge as we enter altered states of consciousness. Of all the methods we have discussed to alter your awareness, sound is one of the most ancient and primeval. Sound touches us with an eloquent and universal language that speaks to our very cells.

The Upanishads of ancient India say that in the beginning the god Brahma uttered the sound *Om,* and out of this the universe came into being. Through this creative force all things are related, no matter how seemingly different.

In Genesis, we find the same basic concept: In the beginning was the Word, and the Word said, Let there be light. It is also written in Genesis that we were created in the image of God. In this mythos, we have some of the same creative power as the first Creator.

We are, all of us without exception, continually re-creating our world through the power of sound. For better or worse, we use this power whenever we speak or think a thought, for all thoughts and feelings set into motion movements of energy.

Vibration is the primordial language of creation. And we cannot avoid the fact that we create and re-create our lives through this power. Our power to think and to speak can birth or destroy whole nations and nurture friendships or lay them to waste. Positive self-talk can inspire and motivate us. Negative self-talk can depress us and make us ill. The power of the brain to speak to itself and others is a remarkable ability.

We use this power everyday, therefore we take it for granted. If we understood the vast repercussions of our thoughts and words, we might be more attentive to them.

I have seen a child's wonder crushed by a parent's harsh words, and I have seen a person in agony given solace by a few kind words in passing.

In the mythic world where the gods live and breathe, Brahma is still continually re-creating the universe. To each of us he has given a small part of his power to create. With this power we can create heaven or hell. The choice and the responsibility is with each one of us.

CHAPTER FOURTEEN

Quantum Mind: The Land Where Magic Lives

"It don't mean a thing if it ain't got that swing."
— Duke Ellington and Irving Mills

I was quite tired one evening after spending a long day working on an intensive project involving brain performance. The project required that I create a series of complex exercises that would work with major structures in the brain through sound and imagery.

As I recall, I was sitting at a traffic light. The sun had just slipped below the horizon, setting the low hung clouds on fire with brilliant reds and oranges.

After months of work, I had come upon the last tape in the series and I was completely stumped. I had no idea of how to proceed. For several days and nights, I had wrestled with the problem of how to proceed during one of the crucial transitions in the exercise.

Exasperated, I sat at the red light watching five o'clock traffic pour into the main thoroughfare. The flow of cars seemed hypnotic, and I felt myself entering an unusual mental space.

Time seemed to stretch out and slow down. Things seemed more real and three dimensional. In an instant, my thoughts turned to that tape again for the hundredth time. But instead of grappling with the problem, I just sat with it as I watched the line of cars and the brilliant red and orange clouds floating across the ever darkening sky.

I suddenly knew, although I did not know how I knew, the solution to the problem. I understood, in that moment, that all I had to do was wait and let the solution emerge.

My eyes were caught by a beautiful butterfly with golden wings about thirty yards off to the right side of my car. I watched it, transfixed, as it came and sat on the windshield of my car, directly in front of my forehead.

I had the distinct feeling that the butterfly had flown to me for a reason, that it was not a random occurrence. It had given me the answer to my problem.

Now, rationally speaking there is no evidence that was the case. But emotionally and intuitively I felt the butterfly had come in response to my dilemma.

The incident reminds me of a story about Carl Jung. According to the story the psychiatrist was working with a patient in Zurich in the middle of winter. His patient was recounting a personally significant dream which involved a bumble bee. As Jung listened to his patient both of them heard a thump at the window. As Jung looked to his window, he saw, incredible as it may seem, a bumble bee trying to get into the office.

Jung experienced many such episodes that seemingly violated rationality. He called these types of experiences "synchronicities." Synchronicities occur when there is a powerful movement within the psyche that parallels an event in the outer reality.

I have experienced many synchronicities with my clients as they entered altered states of consciousness. Something about the deeper brain states seems to increase the frequency of these kinds of events.

Once many years ago while I was involved with intensive inner work, I began to journal with a dream figure that had been haunting my dreams for several weeks. In the dreams, he would stand outside my back porch in the shadows at night. As I stepped out of the house he would shoot me down with a submachine gun.

In Jungian terms, the house is a symbol of the self, thus I took the dreams to be a message about stepping out of my self into the world. This was, in fact, the issue I was dealing with in my outer life.

I had named the dream saboteur Liz since he looked remarkably like some kind of lizard. One morning around three o'clock, I was journaling with Liz when the phone rang. It was a long distance phone call and you could hear the crackling of static in the background. I still vividly remember being riveted to the phone as the other party asked "Is Liz there?"

My rational mind went nuts. The odds against getting a wrong phone number for someone named Liz at three in the morning, just as I was journaling with a dream image named Liz, must have been astronomical.

Immediately after that incident the dreams stopped. Somehow the issue of being in the world seemed more resolved. Had the movement within my own psyche at three o'clock in the morning drawn someone who knew a Liz to make a phone call and dial the wrong number, getting me instead? Such ideas simply do not make sense in our logically based way of viewing things.

A new paradigm is needed here – another map of reality.

The Map of Quantum Physics

Between each of the billions of neurons within our brains, there are little gaps. These gaps, called synapses, are microscopic in size and occur just as the axon of one nerve cell reaches out to touch the dendrite of its neighbor. (To refresh your memory on this, review Chapter 3.)

As you may recall, all nerve impulses have to jump this little gap in order to get to the next neuron. In my opinion, the size of this gap is one of the most important and undiscussed measurements in neuroanatomy. The gap, you see, is about one millionth of an inch across. A very small space indeed, and it is within this distance that the laws of quantum mechanics first begin to appear.

Quantum mechanics applies to extremely small objects.

In the everyday world in which we live, things like billiard balls, tables, cars, rockets, and so on are pretty predictable. If you leave the kitchen one evening with a melon sitting on the table, chances are that the melon will still be on the table when you return in the morning. These laws of motion and rest are collectively called Newton's laws, and as legend has it the fall of an apple suggested to Sir Isaac the train of thought that led to the laws of gravity.

The same force of gravity that holds your melon on the table pulled Newton's apple from its tree more than three hundred years ago.

Newton's laws are great at predicting what happens to objects in our everyday world. Take that melon, for instance, and throw it against the wall. Newton's laws will accurately predict where it will wind up based on calculations from its speed and direction. The same laws apply to everything from automobiles racing down a turnpike to missiles fired into enemy territory to babies being bumped up and down on their father's knee.

But a whole different world emerges we enter the realm where objects are smaller than one millionth of an inch across. This is the realm of atoms and subatomic particles.

If our everyday world were bound by the laws of quantum mechanics, things would not be so predictable. There would be no strong probability, as in our world, that the melon you left on the table would be there in the morning. You might, for instance, walk into the kitchen to find the melon floating in the middle of the room and the kitchen table attached to the ceiling. And if you were to take a knife to cut the melon for breakfast, you could not guarantee that the knife would ever make it to the melon. It might turn into a liquid and spill onto the floor, or the molecules of which it is made might scatter like sand, leaving you holding air. And if, out of frustration, you were to pick up that melon and throw it towards the wall, Newton's laws would be useless. You could not predict where it would land. You could only come up with a probability of where it might land. It could for instance, smash right into the wall as usual, or fly up and hit the ceiling, or explode in mid air into a trillion particles each one careening off in its own direction. It could even burst into light and disappear from the room in waves of incandescence. You can imagine the horror or amusement, depending on your mood, of living in such a world.

The quantum universe is a weird place. We do not know with certainty anything about the movement of subatomic particles. Here there are only probabilities.

This uncertainty of things in the quantum realm is so important, it even has a title: Heisenburg's Uncertainty Principle. We will come back to this again when we discuss human behavior.

Another key concept in quantum physics is Bell's Theorem. According to Bell's Theorem, there is no such thing as an objective observer of quantum events. The very act of observation affects the results. One of the more common ways this is experienced is in the collapsing of a probability.

Now hold on to your hats, this really gets weird. In the quantum realm, objects may take the form of either a particle or a wave. We cannot say with certainty whether something is a particle or a wave until we observe it. But Bell's Theorem says that as soon as we observe it, we have affected it. In other words, if we are looking for a wave, the phenomena will take the form of a wave, and if we are looking for a particle, that is what we will see. So much for Aristotelian logic!

There are even more oddities in the quantum realm, but let's take a look at the ramifications of these two principles first.

You probably remember that at the tip of each axon there are a group of molecules called neurotransmitters. These little puzzle pieces, when stimulated properly, jump across the chasm of the synapse to receptor sites at the tip of the waiting dendrite. Because the transmission of the signal from one neuron to the next requires an exquisite matching of neurotransmitters to receptor sites, the whole system gets rather precarious.

If the neurotransmitter molecules were in the realm of Newton's laws, we could predict with certainty where these crucial puzzle pieces would land, and we could say with a good deal of certainty if the stimulus were to continue on its pathway to the brain. But remember, this is not Newton's world. This is the quantum world with all of its uncertainty. Thus we cannot predict with certainty that a neurotransmitter will correctly stimulate the tip of its waiting dendrite. And since much, if not all of our perception and awareness depends upon these myriads of neuronal interactions, we cannot predict what we will experience either.

This means no one can predict with certainty anything about

perception.

Something that happened just a few moments ago while I was writing will serve my point beautifully. My sons Chris and Jeremy were calling my name. Evidently they called several times, but I did not hear them. My attention was on something else. What I would have normally perceived I did not.

"Didn't you hear us call you?" they asked in agitation as they walked into my office.

"No, I didn't," was my reply.

"Umph..." was theirs.

We had just received a lesson in the uncertainty of perception. Within the biochemical sea of my own nervous system, the signal of their voices calling my name was, for awhile, unable to break into my conscious awareness.

The next time you are in a conversation with someone, do not automatically assume that they heard, much less understood you. The randomness of perception is always at work, even if you do not recognize it.

To be human is to live in two worlds, the world of Newton's laws and those of quantum mechanics. While our bodies obey the laws predicted by Newton, our minds are of another realm altogether.

Just as our own neurotransmitters are caught in the warp of quantum space, our minds are filled with uncertainty and unpredictability. Humans, by nature, are surprising creatures. I feel that much of this uncertainty comes from the very fact that the physical basis of our experience is firmly rooted in the quantum events of our own nervous systems.

Although Bell's Theorem is usually applied only to events within the world of subatomic particles, it readily applies to our minds and behavior as well.

I recall a rather remarkable story about a teacher in one of the large inner city schools. Statistically most of the students in this school would either drop out, be on welfare, and/or go to prison.

For some mysterious reason this particular teacher's students were doing the impossible. Almost all of them were graduating from that same high school and many of them were going on to college. When asked by school officials about her "secret," she replied "Oh... I just love them as if they were my own." The love and attention from this one teacher had done what millions of dollars pumped into an ineffective school system had been unable to do.

I believe that this teacher and her students were experiencing the results of Bell's Theorem. She was looking for talent and courage in her students. That was what she found, and through her vision of what they could be, their views of themselves and what they could accomplish were changed as well.

As in education, the field of psychology is especially susceptible to Bell's Theorem. In a fairly well known study, a group of psychology students were admitted to a mental institution for "observation." The attending doctors were not told that this was a study, rather they were told that this group of patients had been previously diagnosed as schizophrenic. The students had been told to just act normal. In the assessment of these students, the attending psychologists all verified the original diagnosis they had been led to believe even though previous diagnosis by the researchers had noted all of the subjects as "normal."

Had the learned doctors at the institution merely seen what they had expected to see?

It is fairly well accepted in corporate psychology that employees respond to what is expected of them. If they are rewarded for being motivated and interested in the needs of the company, they will do better than employees who are just expected to do the minimum. Management's view of its workers will inexorably shape what type of workers they have.

There are two other oddities about the quantum world I would like to discuss in the context of altered states. They are the twin paradoxes of time and space.

If you take two particles and bump them into each other, they will begin to spin. If these two particles spin off in separate directions they will, of course, be separated by space. If you cause one of the separated particles to spin in the opposite direction, immediately the other particle will also spin in the opposite direction. This theory has been verified by scientific observation. How do they do this?

Our concepts of time and space are violated by this odd happening. If these two particles are actually somehow in communication, it should require some time for them to "talk" with each other. But such would not seem to be the case from these results. The change of direction in one particle immediately elicits a change in the other particle. Time collapses. It is instantaneous.

The world of quantum mechanics is so exceedingly complex we cannot begin to adequately describe it. Besides, most of quantum mechanics must be expressed in the language of mathematics. But for our purposes, we can glean enough to present a plausible view of what may be happening in altered states of consciousness.

I called this chapter "Quantum Mind: The Land Where Magic Lives" because it is through the map of quantum physics that we can begin to explain some of the things that happen during altered states of consciousness.

If you have been going through the development exercises in this book, you have by now experienced altered states of awareness.

You will have noticed that as you enter the more relaxed

states, time undergoes a transformation. Your usual sense of time somehow alters, either speeding up or considerably slowing down. In a dream for instance, one could experience the passage of years when in objective time it only took a few minutes.

In altered states of consciousness, our sense of space also changes dramatically. You may have noticed as you did some of the exercises that you had "floaty feelings" or a sense that you were spinning or that space was expanding or contracting. Our sense of space is generated from within our own consciousness, and in altered states of awareness this sense of space becomes fluid and malleable just as in the world of quantum mechanics.

In our everyday world, we cannot walk through walls or instantaneously teleport to a distant city or time. There are reputedly people who can do such things (called siddhas) but for most of us this is an impossibility, at least in waking state. However, in an altered state of consciousness such as a dream or certain types of inner work, we can indeed walk through walls and instantaneously propel ourselves to distant times and/or locations.

Science is now beginning to document that such experiences can have a powerful and beneficial effect on our bodies and in our waking lives.

In the very first chapter of this book, I shared how a client was able to free herself from pain through a process of internal imagery and music. The events she experienced during her fantasy and the "healing rock" out on the Sedona desert were real.

No, you could not see the rock or desert in her mind. If someone had walked into my office at that moment, they would have seen a woman sitting in a chair listening to my voice and some music in the background. This was the Newtonian reality of that moment.

But the quantum reality of that moment was something very

different. The images in her mind and the feelings of freedom and solace in her body were as real as the chair she was sitting in. But her "inner reality" was of a different order than her outer reality. In the moments of her inner work in my office, time and space had become more fluid, more malleable. Things that could not happen in the Newtonian world where she lived easily occurred with ease and grace in the "inner world" of her experience. She had entered the realm where magic lives, where events not normally possible come true.

She was, after all, dying from cancer and in intense pain constantly. But during her sojourn to this far and distant world within herself she experienced peace, joy, and freedom from pain.

You, too, can have access to your own "inner world" of magic where the impossible can happen.

I am reminded of a situation several years ago when I worked with a woman in deep grieving. Her son had died unexpectedly and the loss had been devastating. As I guided her into a receptive brain state, I suggested that she would be able to go to the place where her son was and be with him once again.

Immediately the woman's face showed an incredible and ineffable joy as she looked upward. Tears of joy fell from her closed eyes. I did not know what had happened until it was over, and we had a chance to talk.

Jesus had appeared to her, and, taking her hand, he had guided her to what she described as a heavenly world. Here in this land of peace and light she met her son. She experienced being with him for hours although her actual time in "trance" had been about twenty minutes. When she left my office she was in a deep state of peace and joy.

Subsequently her depression and grief lifted. The time she spent with him in her "inner world" had given her the strength to continue living.

The power of her experience stayed with me a long time.

Since that time, I have worked with others from different religious and philosophical persuasions. Many of these people had similarly powerful transformational and transcendent experiences although their guides did not necessarily take the form of Jesus. It seems that the identity of a "higher being" in altered states of consciousness takes a form according to the person's own religious/philosophical beliefs.

Belief is a powerful filter of perception whether it be the perception of an individual or of a group. An incident that occurred on one of Magellan's voyages demonstrates this point in a dramatic manner. As the explorer sailed around the tip of South America, he stopped at a place called Tierra del Fuego, the southernmost point in the Western hemisphere. Coming ashore he met some local natives who had come out to see the strange visitors. What transpired seems hard to imagine, but the ship's historian documented the event.

As Magellan came ashore, the natives asked him how he got there. He pointed out to the full-masted sailing ships at anchor off the coast. Incredible as it seems, none of the natives could see the ships that were clearly visible to Magellan and his crew. The natives had never seen anything like sailing ships. They did not expect to see them, and so they did not see them.

According to the historian's records, the first person to see the ships was the village shaman or witch doctor. He said that if they looked out to the sea from the corner of their eyes they could see something. Finally, everyone in the tribe could see the ships.

Shamans are trained to "see" and work in the inner world of reality. My hunch is that through years of entering trance states and working in his own "inner reality," the shaman's perception was more flexible than the other members of his tribe. Thus he was able to see Magellan's ships even though they violated the consensus reality of his kinsman.

We are all hypnotized by our cultural and social beliefs. Every day our brains filter out perceptions that do not fit in with our expectations. The world is not as constant as we believe it to be.

Altered states of awareness loosen our strangle hold on perception and allow us to see and sense and know things normally not accessible to us.

By entering our own inner worlds we can heal and transform ourselves in remarkable ways. The laws that bind us to our outer world of perception (the Newtonian world) have no hold over us in our inner world. The freedom and uncertainty of quantum reality is "wired" into our very nervous systems.

The atoms and subatomic particles of our universe spin together and move apart, creating all manners of forms and destroying them as well. The giant pulsars in the heavens and mice in autumn fields share something in common with all things including humans. We are all formed from trillions upon trillions of infinitesimally small particles and waves of energy, waves and energy that do not obey the laws of our outer world but which obey laws that challenge our concepts of reality.

Some people will prefer to hold onto their own small island of "reality" pretending that they have the answers to all of life's questions. And when the Magellean ships of new ideas come upon their shores, they will not be able to see them.

But working with altered states of consciousness can help to free limited perceptions of ourselves and the world. With freedom of perception comes new information, new possibilities, and new life.

No one yet knows the limits of what is possible by entering into and working with inner realities. If history is any example, many of our ideas about what is impossible today will be accepted as commonplace tomorrow.

Read over the "expert opinions" below from various authorities at the beginning of the twentieth century. These beliefs of what could or could not be done now seem quaint and humorous, but they were deadly serious at the time.

"Everything that can be invented has been invented."
Charles H. Durell
Director of U.S. Patent Office, 1899

"Who the hell wants to hear actors talk?"
Harry M. Warner
Warner Bros. Pictures, 1927

"Sensible and responsible women do not want to vote."
Grover Cleveland, 1905
U.S. President

"There is no likelihood man can ever tap the power of the atom."
Robert Milikan, 1923
Nobel Prize in Physics

"Heavier than air flying machines are impossible."
Lord Kelvin, 1895
President, Royal Society

What our experts deem improbable today will no doubt suffer a similar fate in the future. The destiny of the human species is accelerating at an incredible rate. If we survive our own growing pains, who knows what we will attain!

I believe that the quantum world of inner experience offers a depth and richness of creative resources to which all of us have access. It is also my belief that we must come to know our own inner world if humanity is to survive.

We can no longer afford to be ignorant of the vast powers that we carry within ourselves.

CHAPTER FIFTEEN

Lucid Dreaming, Insomnia, and Things that Go Bump in the Night

"Our dreams are the stuff that life is made of."
– Will Shakespeare

Our dreams haunt us.

How many times have you awakened from a dream moved by the urgency of its voice, only to find that as you tried to remember it, the thing slipped through your fingers?

In this chapter, I will not only show you how to remember and work with your dreams, I will show you how to become aware of your dreams as they are happening. This phenomenon is often called lucid dreaming.

There is power in this. The ability to alter your dream world can have profound affects on your life.

But before I discuss ways to lasso that wild mare of the night, let's take a look at what science has discovered about when our dreams seem to occur and what is happening in the brain when they do.

Every night when you go to sleep your brain states transit through Alpha, Theta, and into the deepest levels of Delta. These transits are periodic, and sleep researchers have divided our sleep into two major patterns.

Deep sleep or S sleep is characterized by slow wave EEG activity, thus the S. This Delta pattern takes up the bulk of our sleeping time.

A second type of sleep pattern called REM sleep or D sleep is characterized by rapid eye movements (REM) and is often accompanied by dreams, thus the D sleep.

The first episode of REM or D sleep in adults lasts about ten minutes. As sleep continues into the night, the periods of REM sleep increase until by early morning REM sleep may take up as much as an hour.

Babies spend much more time in REM than adults, though the reason is not yet clear.

In terms of EEG activity, sleep may be viewed as a regular process with periodic fluctuations between S sleep (deep sleep) and REM sleep (where dreams occur).

The entire picture is not in yet on the brain mechanisms involved in dreams, but research conducted by Dr. Allan Hoban and Dr. Robert McCorley point to an important area.

Drs. Hoban and McCorley refer to the brain as a "dream generator." In numerous studies, they have detected increased activity in the pons area of the brain during sleep. Their theory is that this activity somehow stimulates the neocortex.

While other structures in the brain are involved in sleep, the neocortex, without question, is a major brain area involved in the production of dream images and experiences..

During the last several decades, sleep researchers have studied thousands of subjects. Their findings indicate that for every 100 persons in REM sleep, over 80 percent will remember a dream if you awaken them. Half of them will report an emotional feeling accompanying the dream and 90 percent will report a visual scene from the dream. Another 50 percent will be able to relate the dream to some recent experiences.

It is clear that REM sleep is a unique brain state, and yet, when we look at its EEG activity it has some similar parallels to waking states. This may partially explain why dreams often seem so real. It's as if REM sleep is mimicking waking state even though all the images are generated from within.

Dreams have an uncanny reality about them. How often have you awakened from a dream that seemed totally real only to suddenly realize you had been duped, that you were not skiing in the Swiss Alps as you had thought, but snuggled up in your bed?

Dreams can also have a strange effect on our waking state. A particularly powerful dream can color our feelings for hours. I remember such a dream I had one winter morning a few years ago. In my dream it was snowing, and I recall walking through the eerie silence of my dream world as it snowed all around me. When I awakened from my dream and looked out the window, it was also snowing. Suddenly all of the feelings from the dream poured into my waking state, and the dream feelings seemed mixed with my waking feelings for most of the morning.

For aeons, man has tried to fathom the power and meaning of the dream worlds. Shamans have used dream experiences as doorways into other dimensions of consciousness, and some modern psychologies, such as Jungian Analysis, use dreams to understand the workings of the psyche.

Dreams have also been known to solve creative problems. Robert Mueller, a former assistant secretary to the United Nations, often uses dreams to help him solve international dilemmas and problems.

The ability of dreams to assist us makes sense when you consider that they reveal workings of the non-dominant hemisphere. Freed from the fetters of our normal day-to-day thinking, we are able, in dreams, to often contact more creative aspects of our brain/minds. If we learn to listen to the language of our dreams we can enrich our lives in remarkable ways.

One way for you to contact your dream world is by keeping a "dream journal." Dreams are tender and embryonic things. They resist logical analysis and quickly fade from our memories upon awakening. Have you noticed that in the process of describing a dream to someone else that the power of it seems to disappear the more you talk about it? Or that you may say to yourself that you will remember the dream upon awakening only to find that all memory of it has totally eluded you?

If you wish to make your dream world more accessible, you may want to keep a notebook (dream journal) by your bed. After you have a dream that seems significant, awaken yourself enough to scribble some sketchy notes about it. Then go back to sleep. This is not a time to necessarily analyze it. You are simply recording enough points about the dream to jog your memory. Then upon awakening, you can look at what you have written and reconstruct your dream.

If you are working on a particular problem or creative challenge, you can program your mind to come up with solutions in the dream state. It may take some time to train yourself to be able to do this, but it is quite possible. Simply write in your dream journal a brief description of the problem or challenge you want help with and then go over it in your mind as you go off to sleep. Say to yourself inwardly something to the effect that you would like help and information with the problem, whatever it is. And then release it. Forget about it and go to sleep. Every time you catch yourself having just dreamed, awaken yourself enough to make some notes in your journal. In the morning read what you have written and see if it sheds any light on your problem.

One thing to remember is that dreams are creative acts. They are often metaphorical rather than logical, and they speak with a richness characteristic of the unconscious mind. I recall a dream I had several years ago when I had asked for help in finding why I had sudden drops in physical energy that left me exhausted by mid-afternoon. In a series of dreams, I experienced myself as a jet pilot soaring over the earth up into the heavens. At the same point in each of the dreams, I reached down for a candy bar and as soon as I took a bite the engine stopped dead and I lost altitude, crashing into a cropping of trees. Although illogical, the dream had addressed my problem eloquently. My consumption of sugar was the culprit and subsequent medical tests revealed that I was hypoglycemic. The solution was to eliminate simple sugars from my diet.

You may need to try the above strategy several times before you get "results," but stick with it. It is not uncommon for some people to take several weeks or so of going through the process every night before they start consciously accessing their dream states.

The dream world is pregnant with life and insight. Unlike our waking state, objects in dreams can talk and the people in our dream world are often metaphors of something else. Often dreams address emotional questions in addition to practical ones.

The technique below is a powerful process that allows you to re-enter a dream and dialogue with its contents for the purpose of gaining a deeper understanding of its significance.

Entering the Dream World

1. Put on the Creative Imagining tape mentioned previously, or some other kind of restful music.

2. Begin to do Noise Removal Breathing for three to five minutes. Follow this by doing one cycle of Level One Breathing.

3. Imagine that you are back in the dream and imagine that you can sense everything as you left it. If you "see" things, imagine "seeing" what you saw in the dream. You may just have a felt sense of things rather than actually seeing anything. This is okay. Just go with the ways of re-experiencing the dream that seem most natural to you.

4. In your imagination, move towards a person, animal, or object that you have some question about. You may for instance ask a person who or what they represent. It is possible for you to talk with them just as you would in a normal waking state. As you speak with this person, animal, or object, he, she, or it may change form or take you on a journey. Feel free to follow, as these inner journeys are often revealing. If, at any time, you feel fearful, image a shield around you. This effective technique immediately communicates to the unconscious mind in a language it clearly understands. To construct a Shield, imagine and feel yourself in the "dream world" surrounded by a cocoon of purest white light. This color is one of the highest vibrational frequencies in the visual spectrum, and it is also a symbol of consciousness itself. This image "brings to light" the true nature of things revealed to you in the dream world.

5. You may find the descriptive process of Image Streaming discussed in Chapter 10 to be useful for retrieving more material.

6. When you feel that you have fully explored your dream and communicated with all of its important figures, record your experience in your dream journal.

Re-entering and exploring your dreams in this way on a regular basis will attune you to the depth and subtleties of your own dream world.

Lucid Dreaming

Perhaps one of the most intriguing of the dream states is something called lucid dreaming. In lucid dreaming, you are not only dreaming, but you are aware that you are dreaming.

It's as if some part of "the mind" is awake and experiencing the dream, knowing that it is a dream. Lucid dreaming can be a very powerful experience.

For instance, while working on a chapter for *Brain States*, I had a lucid dream that powerfully affected my outer waking life.

For the few weeks prior to the dream, I had been struggling with some personal issues. I was under stress and not dealing with it very well.

In the dream I was at some large hospital. The doctors told me that I needed brain surgery. Without it I would die. But even if I underwent the operation, there was a ninety percent chance that it would not be successful. Also, the operation was very expensive, and I couldn't afford it.

During the entire dream I was aware that I was dreaming. At a critical point in the dream, I decided I did not like the experience, and so I chose to heal myself. In the dream I prayed for help and commanded that I be healed.

Suddenly three doctors appeared and worked on me with some kind of laser apparatus. While they were working on me, my body temperature rose — not my dream body mind you, but my physical body. I was perspiring and kicked off the blankets.

When the dream doctors finished their strange operation, my body temperature returned to normal.

What was fascinating about this, besides the alteration in body temperature, was how I felt when I awakened. I felt renewed, somehow cleansed, and in a much better place than I had been for weeks.

The ability to alter dream reality can have powerful and beneficial effects. The key is to become aware of your dreams, to notice that you are dreaming the dream. This rather esoteric seeming ability can be developed.

Numerous shamanic cultures have developed methods to utilize the dream state. The social anthropologist, Carlos Castaneda, conducted a lengthy study of shamanic dream methods used by a group of Mexican sorcerers. These methods involved the shifting of attention while dreaming, which profoundly altered perception.

In one of his books, Castaneda is advised by his teacher to look for his hands or feet in his dreams. By doing so, he is told, he will remember that he is dreaming and have access to using his dream body. The technique does work, and you can try it for yourself, although it will take most people many trials before they actually remember to look at their hands or feet while they are dreaming.

Until the work of Stephen LaBerge, Ph.D., lucid dreaming was considered to be more of a folk tale than an actual state of consciousness. However since 1980, Dr. LaBerge has conducted numerous studies on the effects and benefits of lucid dreaming to the point of formulating methods to increase the likelihood of such dreams occurring. Dr. LaBerge also developed a machine to help persons develop awareness of lucid dream states. In 1988 he formed the Lucidity Institute, an organization committed to continued research in the area of lucid dream states. For information about the Lucidity Institute, and Dr. LaBerge's excellent book, the reader is referred to Appendix C.

I have worked with lucid dream states for several years and found them to be quite helpful in a number of ways. One of the most compelling is the directness with which other parts of my self can communicate with me during such episodes. Creative ideas have also come to me during lucid dream states, and, as I mentioned earlier, they can have positive health benefits as well.

The protocol that follows is a training method that will eventually produce lucid dreams and allow you to experience and work in your "dream body." Ideally it should be practiced in the evening before retiring to bed. By going through the exercise every night for a while, you will increase your chances of experiencing lucid dreams.

Training Protocol for Lucid Dreaming

1. Put on the Creative Imagining tape, if you have a copy, and play it at low volume. Lie down and close your eyes. Lie on your left side if this is comfortable or, if not, gently touch your forefinger to the thumb of each hand and let your hands rest comfortably by your side.

2. As you listen to the tape, begin to do Noise Removal Breathing for two to three minutes. Follow this with Level One Breathing for one complete cycle.

3. Imagine and feel that you have a point of pure white light in the middle of your forehead. Sense it radiating its light both into the front of your brain and directly in front of you.

4. Now imagine and feel that you are walking along a deserted beach at twilight. Look up at the sky and notice the moon and stars. As you walk along this beach sense the point of white light in your forehead and look down at

your hands and feet. Rotate your hands in front of you as you look at them in the light of the moon and the stars.

Next, imagine that you have come to an entrance to some kind of underground cave. As you walk down seven stairs, reach out to open the door and look at your hand before you. As you open the door and walk through the entrance, notice that you are standing in a very large cavernous room with many doors. Feel and sense that there is a wonderful calmness and peace around you as you stand in that room

You will find yourself drawn to one of the doors. As you walk towards that door, know that behind it is something of value or interest to you at this time. As you walk across the room towards the door, notice and feel the point of white light in your forehead and glance down at your hands and feet. When you get to the door, reach out your hand to open the door. Pause and look at your hand. Open the door and explore the room, knowing that the things, persons, and beings you find there may be metaphorical. You may, if you feel drawn to do so, dialogue with any object or being you find there. As you explore the room, occasionally glance at your hands or feet and get a sense of the point of white light in the middle of your forehead.

After you have explored the room to your satisfaction, return to the large room and the entrance that leads to the stairs. Open the door and walk up onto the beach. Bring your awareness back to your physical body, and slowly open your eyes.

For best effect this protocol should be practiced every one or two days until you begin to have lucid dreams. Some people will begin to have lucid dreams quite soon after they begin practicing the Training Protocol. Others may take longer. Be persistent with your training and you will get there.

To increase the likelihood of lucid dreaming, do the following exercise at night when you go to sleep.

Preparation for Lucid Dreaming
1. Lie on your left side, if it is comfortable to do so, just as you did in the Training Protocol. If this position is not comfortable for you, use the finger touching method also discussed in the Training Protocol.
2. Close your eyes and lower your brain state by doing Level One Breathing for one cycle.
3. Imagine and feel a point of white light in the middle of your forehead just like you have previously worked with in the above protocol.
4. As you let your awareness gently rest at this point, silently say to yourself: "I intend to have lucid dreams tonight. I recognize when I am dreaming and I am able to move freely in my dream body." (This statement is only a guide. You may state your intention in any way that you desire.)
5. Continue to keep your mental focus gently at the point of light in the middle of your forehead. When you feel yourself drifting off to sleep, just let go of your focus.

You may change your body position throughout the night as you wish. When you catch yourself dreaming, remember the point of light in your forehead and to look at your hands or feet.

Have patience and enjoy your explorations of the dream world. Eventually you will be conscious while you are dreaming, and with that a whole new world will open before you.

For those who would like a relatively low cost high-tech approach to consciousness, Synetic Systems (Seattle, Washington) is developing a Lucid Dreaming Machine as this book goes to press.

The device uses a combination of bio-feedback and light/ sound pulsing to alert a person when he or she enters REM activity.

According to Dan Claussing, who has coordinated development of the device, the machine assists in the generation of lucid dreams for those who have been trained in the subtleties of the technology. In other words, you probably will not be able to pull the device off the shelf and use it without some kind of training. Still, the idea that a device can be used to trigger the insightfulness of lucid dreaming is an intriguing and useful one.

Insomnia

Sleeplessness may be caused by several different factors such as over excitement, stress, anxiety, stimulants (caffeine), too much to eat or drink, entering another time zone, as well as certain types of mental conditions.

The exercises in this section will allow you to effectively lower your brain state and enter sleep in most instances. There is a caution here.

IMPORTANT: If you have been unable to sleep for several days or weeks and have also been unable to eat and are experiencing severe bouts of depression, anxiety, and/or paranoia you may be in the throws of a severe psychological condition. If you or someone you know is experiencing symptoms like these, immediately seek professional attention from a psychiatrist, psychologist, counselor, or clinic. Such conditions, left unattended, can be dangerous.

Insomnia is characterized by a lot of Beta and High Beta activity. Since sleep is associated with the slow wave pattern of Delta, to get to sleep you must slow down your brain waves. There are several ways to lower your brain state to induce sleep, and I have put them together into two strategies described below.

However, the very first step in moving from insomnia to sleep is to assess your thinking processes. Are you worried about something? Is something bugging you? Often sleeplessness is caused by worries or troubles that we turn over and over again in our minds. This obsessive thinking tends to create Beta and high Beta activity in the brain, which is counter-productive to the slow wave patterns of sleep.

First be clear if there is something appropriate you can actually do to affect the situation at that time. If it is clear that you cannot really deal with the situation until the next day, give it up for the time being. After all, if you are sleep deprived, you will not be in any shape to deal with it.

Of course, this is where the personality of the individual enters the picture. Some people may find it hard to let go of their worries, even for a few hours. If you were such a person at the beginning of this book, and if you have been faithfully practicing the stress management techniques and suggestions in Chapter 8, you will have pleasantly discovered that your control needs are easing, making life easier for both you and those around you.

Once you are clear that you cannot change whatever it is that is bothering you at the moment, you are ready to change your brain state and enter the restful state of sleep.

Getting To Sleep Protocol #1
1. Do the Two Minute Stress Buster (Chapter 8) at least three times and more, if you wish.
2. Lie down, get comfortable and do Noise Removal Breath-

ing for five to ten minutes. As you breathe up through your legs, arms, and torso imagine and feel the breath "swishing" through all areas of tension. As you exhale normally, imagine and feel these tensions leaving your body. Let your breathing be calm, easy, and slow.

3. After you have finished Noise Removal Breathing you will feel a little more relaxed. Now do one cycle of either Level One Breathing or Level Two Breathing. It is all right if you fall asleep in the middle of it. In fact if you do Level Two Breathing, you can just about guarantee that you will not be able to get all the way through it. If you wake up again simply do the breathing again.

This protocol is often effective with light cases of insomnia. If you keep waking up in spite of the breathing, do the Heaven's Gate Meditation Relaxation technique in strategy #2.

Getting To Sleep Protocol #2

Sometimes it is almost impossible to get to sleep, short of medication. In such instances the Heaven's Gate Meditation (Chapter 8) can be a life saver. When flying through international time zones, I have often found myself unable to sleep the night before an important training or talk. By using this technique, I have been able to "rest" throughout the night, even though I may not have truly gone to sleep. The cycles of rest you enter in this strategy are very deep and an hour or so of this can easily refresh and energize you as much as a few hours of sleep.

1. Go through all of the steps in Protocol #1.

2. After you have completed the breathing in Step 3, do the Heaven's Gate Meditation as described in Chapter 8. Ideally you should be practicing this technique regularly so that it comes to you very naturally. (Note: Instead of sitting up as usual, lie down with pillows or blankets by

your side so that you can rest your arms. This way you can hold your hands in the proper manner resting on your chest.)

If you drift off to sleep, as often happens, just enjoy it. If you should come back to conscious awareness, simply begin the meditation again. Continue in this way throughout the night until it is time for you to get up.

When you start your day you will be pleasantly surprised at the level of energy and clarity you have.

Light and Sound Brain Machines

If you are lucky enough to have a light and sound brain synchronizer (see Chapter 16), all you have to do is don your goggles and headphones. EEG studies have verified that such devices can lower brain wave patterns and induce slow wave activity characteristic of sleep.

These machines are certainly as effective as most over-the-counter sleep medications and may be a good substitute for those who wish to avoid taking pharmaceuticals.

I personally prefer those devices that have a dimmer control for the light goggles since bright lights tend to irritate my eyes when I am fatigued.

Psycho-acoustic Tapes

Some psychoacoustic tapes have also been found to be effective for inducing restful states of consciousness, including sleep. The advantage to tapes is that they are less expensive than light and sound machines, are more easily transportable, and can be played on any kind of stereo cassette player. (See Appendix C.)

There are a number of good sleep-inducing tapes on the market and the interested reader should experiment with them. For information concerning psychoacoustic tapes developed by the author, turn to Appendix B.

CHAPTER SIXTEEN

Brain Machines and Psychoacoustic Environments

"Break through to the other side."
— *Jim Morrison*

N o discussion of brain states would be complete without some mention of what is sometimes referred to as "headware." Although these new technologies have emerged at the beginning of the twenty-first century, their basic methodology is rooted in a much earlier time.

From the dawn of pre-history, man discovered that he could open doorways to his "dream world" through the avenue of his physical senses.

Much of shamanism is an orderly attempt to alter consciousness by altering perceived sensory patterns. The pounding of drums, the elaborate movements of tribal dance, and the ecstatic chanting of sound all had their basis in this fundamental understanding.

With the advent of modern micro-electronics, virtually anyone can have access to this powerful sensory alteration technology. There has been a veritable explosion in the use of these high-tech methods over the last few years, and the trend shows no sign of diminishing.

Some have likened this technology to the early days of personal computers when computer "hacks" were turning out strange machines that could do things no one thought possible. This early phase of the technology bore little resemblance to today's sophisticated industry. And I suspect that we will see a similar evolution of these mind expanding technologies over the next several years.

In this chapter I would like to touch on two broad categories of devices: brain machines and psycho-acoustic environments.

Brain Machines

There are currently two broad categories of headware: 1) light/sound machines and 2) electromagnetic devices. There are also some new hybrids that combine both forms of stimulation.

Light and sound machines alter awareness by directly stimulating the visual and auditory pathways of the brain. In addition, research indicates that the RAS (Reticular Activating System) is probably involved as well. The RAS is a vast network of neural fibers that extends suffusely throughout the brain. It scans for novel stimuli and either alerts or sedates the brain depending on the nature of the stimulus.

In light and sound machines, a light source (usually LEDs) is pulsed at different frequencies depending on the brain state desired.

The brain is extremely sensitive to light, due to the fact that a large cortical neural network is dedicated to vision. Pulsations of light tend to affect both the alert-state of the brain and cortical activity within the neocortex.

A simple primitive experiment will give you a sense of this. Notice your current level of relaxation/alertness. Now, look at some kind of light source and begin to blink your eyes about once every second (1 cps). Do this for a minute or two and notice what happens to your state of relaxation/alertness.

You will, most likely, notice an increase in relaxation and a decrease in alertness. This change in brain state was a direct result of blinking your eyes at about one cycle per second (low Delta).

In light and sound machines, this pulsation of light is handled electronically. In the majority of these machines, the pulsation of light is also coordinated with a pulsing tone. In other words, if the light is pulsing at 4 cps, an audible tone will pulse at 4Hz. This dual entrainment is more powerful than either sound or light by itself.

Extensive EEG and behavioral studies from numerous sources all confirm that light and sound machines affect brain state in quantifiable and measurable ways.

By far the most common use of light and sound machines, at present, is in the area of personal relaxation and self-exploration. However, a growing number of clinicians and educators are finding a much wider range of applications.

Dr. Ramma Sommers has developed a highly successful method of using light and sound machines with learning disabled children. The devices, when used in conjunction with her program, seem to improve both behavior and learning. Synetic Systems (Seattle, Washington) makes a sophisticated and user friendly light and sound machine that integrates directly into any IBM compatible computer. The PC Synchronizer gives the user maximum flexibility including alteration of sound wave forms. In tandem with the Biomedical Operating System (BOS), the PC

Synchronizer can be used to conduct EEG training/feedback sessions with great accuracy. As a result of these advances, a growing number of clinicians are using the device successfully in the treatment of depression and post trauma cases. Based on tentative reports from these therapists, this particular combination of technologies has been quite effective where other methods have failed.

Moving from light and sound stimulation, we find a whole array of devices that use electromagnetics in order to stimulate the brain into altered activity. In CES (Cranial Electrical Stimulation) an electrical signal is pulsed into the brain at low amperage. If the signal is pulsed at 4 cps it tends to increase brain wave activity in the neighborhood of 4Hz. These CES devices are being used in the treatment of chronic pain and in the treatment of addictions with remarkable effectiveness. In fact, CES devices have been approved by the FDA for a number of conditions.

In addition to CES, an array of new devices using electromagnetic fields are being developed both in the United States and in Europe. These machines pulse magnetic fields into the brain, to alter brain wave activity. In assessing the effects of CES and magnetic devices, it would seem that these forms of stimulation are more direct: the form of stimulation is similar to the actual electrical and magnetic signals generated by the brain itself. In light and sound machines, the stimulation is of a sensory nature and is "translated" by the brain into its electrical and magnetic language.

Does this make CES and magnetic devices superior to light and sound machines? There is no conclusive proof, at this time, that either form of stimulation is better than the other. I expect that we will come to better understand the positive benefits and limitations of each kind of stimulation over the next few years. And I suspect that we will also see multiple signal machines being created to take advantage of the potentials inherent in each type of stimulation.

There is a note of caution when it comes to light and sound machines. Generally speaking, a person with a history of epileptic seizures or brain trauma should not use these devices without supervision. The likelihood is small, but the combination of complex visual and auditory patterns could set off a seizure in some patients.

Some people who do not have a history of seizures occasionally experience shaking of limbs and sometimes of the whole body. These are not true seizures and are of no medical concern or danger. Rather, they are often the release of chronic tension held in the muscles. Sometimes they seem to result from an increase of neural activity in the motor areas of the brain, and I have observed that these types of releases often occur parallel with moments of emotional insight.

There is no question that for its ease of use and availability, light and sound machines offer the would-be explorer of consciousness a relatively low cost, safe, and reliable method for altering brain states.

Psychoacoustic Environments

In light and sound machines, a pulsing tone helps to alter brain wave patterns. This tone, which usually matches the frequency of the pulsing light, is routed by the brain's neural network into the auditory cortex.

If the sound pattern emitted by a light and sound machine were likened to a "trickle" of acoustic energy, then psychoacoustic environments create tidal waves!

They do this in a number of ways, depending on the device, but they all share something in common. They all generate Psycoacoustic Immersion Fields (PIFs).

In a PIF you usually lie down or sit up in a special bed or recliner. This bed/recliner often has speakers embedded in it and/or may have speakers situated around it. Music is then played in such a way that your entire body "hears" or resonates to the sound. The effect is dramatic and cannot really be imagined until you have experienced it.

Theoretically, PIFs catalyze a wide band of neural activity due to the fact that both the auditory pathways and the peripheral nerve endings of the body are being stimulated. In other words, you not only hear the music with your ears, but you feel the music with your body.

The applications for psychoacoustic environments are numerous. The Somatron, for example, is a sound table that resonates through specially designed speakers. It is being used in rehabilitation clinics to relax patients and is sometimes used to calm children during chemotherapy. It is also being used by some psychotherapists in the treatment of a number of conditions, including multiple personality disorders. A growing number of massage therapists also use the Somatron™ because it helps relax the client.

Some environments, such as the Rest Rider™, have been developed to stand alone without an operator. The Rest Rider is unique in that it uses a gel cushion (the same kind used by astronauts) to gently support the listener. It also has a TV monitor in the hood that can send visual messages and images to the user. The Rest Rider is being developed primarily for medical environments where the healing power of music can assist patients in their process of recovery. Some sports psychologists have also shown an interest in the device as a means to relax and motivate athletes.

An interesting twist on psychoacoustic environments is the Vibrasound™. The Vibrasound is basically a water bed with special transducers placed underneath the mattress. These transducers vibrate the water as well as the person lying on top of the bed. Headphones are most often used to hear the music, and some practitioners add peripherals such as light/sound machines and tone generators. In the hands of a sensitive operator the Vibrasound can create powerful transpersonal-type experiences. In the right context, such experiences can be a source of tremendous insight and self-understanding.

A while back, I had the pleasure of experiencing the power of the Vibrasound with Chris Boyd, one of the world's foremost Vibrasound trainers. In addition to the Vibrasound, Chris uses a combination of a light/sound machine, a tone generator, and a bank of cassette players and CDs. He also increases the oxygenation of the brain at the beginning of a session by feeding oxygen to the listener for the first few minutes.

The results of this modern alchemy were spectacular. I found myself within a few minutes swimming through cool water. I had entered my own dream world. For the next hour, I interacted with archetypal figures and images from my unconscious mind. The messages these beings gave me were direct and full of meaning for me at that time in my life. The fact that I knew the ins and outs of this technology did not reduce its impact. This modality of inner exploration is, without a doubt, full of possibilities and promise.

There are many advances taking place in the area of psychoacoustic environment both in terms of hardware and application. A notable example of this, in my estimation, are devices based on a technique called "physioacoustic therapy." This methodology involves the use of low frequency sound and was initially developed by Petri Lehikoinen, a Finnish clinical psychologist and music therapist.

Persons undergoing physioacoustic therapy often report that

tense muscles relax and localized pain diminishes or is elimi-
nated completely. Furthermore healthy color often returns to
extremities with circulatory problems.

Lehikoinen and a team of physicians and engineers spent
more than ten years developing a delivery system that could
reliably control the low frequency vibrations that were needed
for physioacoustic therapy. The resulting device is a reclining
chair equipped with a computer and six speakers. The computer
controls the sound while the speakers create the appropriate
psycoacoustic immersion field (PIF). Persons using the device
feel the sound as a "sympathetic resonance within muscles and
other soft tissues."

The device is being marketed in the U.S. under the name Next
Wave. The company distributing the device is authorized to
make three medical claims for the system: it increases vascular
and lymphatic circulation, it reduces pain in areas where it is
applied, and it relaxes muscles. (Note: Further information about
the device may be obtained from Quantum Link. See Appendix
B.)

The two granddaddies of psychoacoustic environments are
currently the Betar™ and the Genesis™. These two devices differ
in many ways, but both of them use a complex interfacing of
technologies. Due to their size and their cost, these environments
are usually purchased by clinics or research centers. Peter Kelly,
the genius behind the Betar, recently developed a smaller version
called the Baby Betar. It is much more affordable for individuals
and requires much less space to operate.

One of the main applications of the Betar and Genesis machines is in the treatment of stress and chronic pain. These
devices can also facilitate powerful inner experiences in the
hands of a sensitive and well-trained operator.

A few years ago while taking "a ride" on the Betar, I had a

powerful experience similar to the one I had on the Vibrasound. In this experience, I entered the cosmic realm and experienced myself hurtling through space. As I entered the center of the galaxy, I felt it trying to communicate with me. Suddenly a flood of tears came to my eyes as I felt a flow of information and images come to me from the galactic core. My cognitive functions were operating well enough for me to recognize that the music had reached a crescendo just at the moment of "breakthrough."

It seems to me that the nature of the experience one has in psychoacoustic environments is greatly dictated by the nature of one's own inner conflicts and resolutions at the time. Experiences in such environments are complex events stemming from one's own psychological make-up, the choice of music, the frequencies that may be played underneath the music and, of course, the type of hardware being used.

We will no doubt see some major advances in the area of psychoacoustic environments during the next few years. And I suspect we will also discover more sophisticated ways to use their potential.

CHAPTER SEVENTEEN

A Map for Explorers
of Consciousness

"The ways of the Creator are not our ways," Mr. Deasy said.
"All history moves toward one great goal, the manifestation of God."
– James Joyce, Ulysses

This chapter deals with material that may or may not be of interest to the reader at this time. It is about super-states of consciousness that transcend current ideas of reality. The types of experiences I discuss fall within the confines of Transpersonal Psychology.

My reason for including this information is that throughout all sectors of society more and more people are having transcendental experiences. The emergence of this heightened "spirituality," for lack of a better term, can be quite forceful. When these states breakthrough into the consciousness of one who is ill-prepared to understand them, it can be quite difficult. It is my hope that the material in this chapter will help both individuals and mental health professionals better understand the process of transcendental states.

The map I am about to discuss is, at this time, my best guess as to how super-states of consciousness are laid out in relation to our normal day-to-day states of awareness.

A map is not the territory. The purpose of a map is to guide a traveler into the territory. Studying a map without entering the territory is like going to a restaurant and eating the menu.

Lost in Sedona

During the last few months of her difficult marriage, Caressa began to experience communications from other beings during her meditations. These beings identified themselves as extraterrestrials and had many things to say to her about the planet, humankind's future, and specifically her future.

These space beings told her that she had been chosen for a grand experiment, and that they would be coming to physically pick her up in a few weeks. She was advised to make plans.

The problem was that the rendezvous point given by the beings was over two thousand miles away. So, selling everything she had, Caressa packed up her car with a small tent, some warm clothes, and headed west for Sedona, Arizona, in the middle of December.

She had carefully calculated the amount of money she would need for her brief sojourn to the desert and gave the rest of her money away to friends and charity.

Arriving to the rendezvous point deep in the desert Caressa set up her tent and waited. Two weeks came and went, no sign of the space ship.

Caressa desperately went into meditation and asked her contacts about the delay. She could not find them. Day after day, night after night, she pleaded with them for an answer: nothing.

Two more weeks came and went. They did not come.

Finally, hungry, exhausted and cold, Caressa left the desert and headed back east.

Caressa had, unwittingly, become a victim of her own non-dominant brain. She had interpreted the deep and rich metaphors from this part of her consciousness as real.

I am not saying that extraterrestrial consciousnesses (i.e. alien intelligences) are not real. I am saying that in Caressa's case they were not real: as verified by their no-show.

Over the years, I have seen many clients who have had spontaneously deep and powerful experiences of altered reality. Some of these people have been greatly enriched by these experiences while others have been devastated by them.

Several years ago, I received a frantic phone call from a personal growth trainer. During one of his five-day intensive training seminars a woman named Sherry had entered a powerful altered state of awareness and had been unable to come out of it.

During (and for several days after) the experience she was filled with a deep universal love for everyone and everything. Out on the grounds of the training facility, she openly wept at the beauty of the trees.

Concerned about her safety, her husband, who also participated in the seminar, made arrangements for their family physician to meet them at the airport when they arrived home.

At the air departure terminal, Sherry had another peak experience and saw everyone in the building surrounded by a beautiful golden light. Stopping at a newsstand, she briefly flipped through a magazine where she saw a picture of the Virgin Mary.

Overcome by an overwhelming love for the female archetype, Sherry went through another metamorphosis. As the Blessed Madonna herself, Sherry started to bless people as her husband escorted her to the plane.

Once on the plane and filled with a divine love and a sense of forgiveness, Sherry ala Madonna recounted to her astonished husband a long history of her infidelity and how she had burned down the family business because she had not wanted to work there anymore.

It was at about this point that the plane reached a cruising altitude of 30,000 feet. Convinced that she could fly, Sherry took off one of her high heeled shoes and began to bang on the window trying to break the plexiglass. Flight attendants quickly subdued her. And when her plane landed, she was whisked off to a sanatorium under police escort.

Standard psychiatric and psychological evaluation views both of these episodes as psychotic in nature. Many therapists view every aspect of these experiences, en masse, as dysfunctional and such persons in desperate need of treatment.

In the course of this chapter, I hope to show that this is not the case. Some aspects of these experiences are explainable in terms other than psychosis or other mental disorders. True, some of the symptoms were indicative of a disintegration of the self and were danger signs. Other symptoms, however, point to a much larger and positive realm of human experience. In other words, the experience of universal love that Sherry experienced is not in the same category as her trying to break open the window of an airplane because she thought she could fly.

I will go into this in more detail a little later, but for now I would like to present a model of consciousness. I believe that this model will allow us to explain how profound altered states of consciousness relate to our normal day-to-day type experience.

It is my belief that many of the experiences people have in profound altered states of awareness are potentially beneficial. The crucial question is whether these experiences can be integrated into the person's psyche or not.

The Spiral of Consciousness

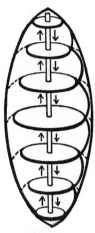

Figure 13

I refer to the figure above as the "Spiral of Consciousness."

You will see that it spirals upwards from a point at the bottom of the spiral expanding and contracting again into another point at the top. There are a total of seven levels of consciousness in this model.

The first four levels are "egoic states" of consciousness, meaning that we have a personal sense of self. However, as we move upwards into the spiral, we lose self identity due to the enormity of the forces and energies we experience in these higher levels.

The ego is a fixed structure within the psyche and shares the same fate as all fixed structures: death. Death to the ego can come as a shattering experience in life such as the loss of a loved one, an accident, intense illness, drugs, and also through the use of spiritual technologies, such as certain types of yogas and austere lifestyles. Even if one survives these without ego dissolution, death of the physical body will, in the end, take away the sense of a personal self.

Let me be more precise about what I mean when I say a personal self. I have, as do you, many identities. I am a father, a husband, a psychotherapist, a musician, a researcher. I have darkish hair, and I like the ocean. I also like animals. I do not like turnips or brussel sprouts, nor do I like accounting. The list goes on. These are all personal likes and dislikes.

These likes and dislikes make me what I am as a personality. Sometimes, depending on my state of mind, I may be very attached and expend a tremendous amount of energy in order to secure something I like and avoid something I dislike.

My personal sense of self is also defined by what I do. At the level of doing, what I do defines who I am.

This is why vacations and retirement are difficult for many people, especially workaholics. Their sense of personal self becomes identified with what they do and when they find themselves in a situation where they can't do what they usually do, they don't know what to do with themselves. And on a deeper ontological level they do not know who they are. This loss of personal identity or personal self can even be a health threat.

Insurance actuary tables show that many people die within a short time of retirement. It is as if, without their job, they have no reason to live.

All of these factors, likes and dislikes, and our personal identity (as defined by what we do) comprise the ego. And yet the ego is more than this. Take away everything I like and prevent me from doing what I do, and you will have a very unhappy camper, but my ego or sense of self will still be intact. I will still know that I am an individual.

The ego is that spark of awareness within us that knows that we are ourselves and endeavors to insure that we survive. In egoic states of consciousness, we experience that we are separate from others to a greater or lesser extent.

In the Spiral of Consciousness, you will see that there are four egoic states of consciousness. Thus, in these first four states of awareness we have a sense of our personal identity. However, the personal identity experienced in level four is vastly different than that experienced in level one.

Level one is the most contracted egoic state. A person in this level experiences themselves as isolated from others. He feels totally separate and feels no connection or compassion to other persons or beings. He is often paranoid and anti-social.

There are health risks associated with level one awareness. These include mental disorders such as depression, substance abuse, suicidal tendencies, and criminal activities. A rapist, for instance, does not feel connection to nor compassion for his or her victim.

Level four awareness, however, is vastly different. At this level of consciousness one experiences powerful expansive forces. It is simply not possible, at level four, to experience the contractive states of level one. There is still a sense of self, but barely. One is typically absorbed in extremely intense emotion such as overpowering universal love and/or a great sense of peace and calm.

Many of the mystics such as Meister Eckhart and some Christian saints, as well as saints and mystics from other traditions, have experienced this level of consciousness.

From this level on up through the spiral we have to use poetry and metaphor to explain the experiences because they are so far removed from our everyday world.

To a person at level four awareness it is as if he or she were on a mountain top and from this high vista looks down with a deep and abiding love for all beings with equal compassion.

There is a sense of personal identity at level four but it is strained. One's personal identity begins to shift from oneself to include all beings as part of the self. This puts undo pressure on the psychic structure of an individual's consciousness.

It is at the edge of level four that a person begins to lose their sense of personal identity. And if one is not prepared for such an experience it can be overwhelming.

The saints and mystics speak of being absorbed in God, taken up as it were into the heavenly realms and while in this state having no distinct sense of self. It is only when they returned to the lower levels that their sense of identity returned.

Which brings us back to the ego. Level one may be viewed as an unhealthy egoic state, while level two moves us into the healthy ego.

The difference between level one and level two is the degree of contraction. In level two, personal identity has expanded to include others such as family members, others in the community and so on. One understands, at level two, that one's own needs do not automatically surpass others' needs. At this level of consciousness we still have a separate sense of self, however, it is more malleable. We can attend to our own needs while also caring for others, if it is appropriate. This is the picture of the "model citizen," responsible for himself or herself, while helpful to others within the community.

A person pausing before a traffic light to allow another car in line is an example of level two awareness. Since the light is red the driver knows that he or she isn't losing anything by letting the other car through.

A person operating from level one awareness, however, would never let another car through. The contraction of the psyche in level one awareness would simply not allow such a spacious and gracious gesture.

Moving upward along the spiral we enter level three awareness. At this level the sense of self is greatly expanded to include "other than self." A common occurrence of this level can be found between some parents and their children. A parent may so identify with the child's needs that the child's needs take precedence. The parent may go hungry in order that the child might eat. The parent may go without a new coat so that the child can have a toy for Christmas. There are many accounts where parents have jeopardized their own lives in order to save the lives of their children.

At level three awareness, one becomes more identified with life itself. Some have the experience in this state of being lived by life, not having a life, but being an expression of life itself. I have observed that it is also at this level of egoic awareness that persons do things that seem highly altruistic.

I had a personal experience with this state many years ago. As an undergraduate student I was experimenting with various spiritual techniques from both the Christian and yogic traditions. During one particular phase of this exploration, I unexpectedly entered a "high level three" state of awareness.

I felt flooded by a deep sense of universal love for complete strangers, children, and animals. The intensity of this love would often bring me to tears of joy. For about a week during this period I found myself in the most unpredictable situations.

One morning around three o'clock, I had a conversation with a stranger on a street corner. She was about my age, about twenty at the time, and very distraught. She was contemplating suicide because she had been robbed. She was convinced that no one cared about her and was surprised that I showed any interest in her plight. I reached into my pocket and handed her all the money I had on me at the time, a little more than a hundred dollars. I told her it was a gift and not a loan.

The look on her face changed from grief and loss to one of hope. I wished her well and left. I had so fully identified with her that I had willingly given away something that was mine to a total stranger. It simply seemed the appropriate thing to do at the moment. I did not think about it. This is characteristic of level three awareness, especially as it begins to move up into level four.

Several years later when I needed three hundred dollars to get my car repaired, she appeared on the very same street. She said that she had hoped to find me. It seems that by giving her that one hundred dollars a few years earlier, it had changed her life. She had moved back home and eventually married. She handed me three hundred dollars in way of saying thanks.

The altruism common to level three may be hard for some to swallow, particularly those clinicians working with co-dependents.

Co-dependency, for those unfamiliar with the term, is a kind of "psychological symbiosis or parasitism" that appears as love and concern for the other person.

Co-dependents often, though not always, develop out of an attempt to cope with drug and/or alcohol addicted families. The co-dependent person basically feels that he or she has little or no intrinsic worth. As children, they often had to be the family hero taking care of others in the family. Thus they become the consummate caregivers. But this caregiving is not out of a real sense of love, it is more a kind of pseudo-love that masks over their real motivation. A co-dependent believes that if they can give enough to another person, he or she will earn that person's love or approval. The thought of another disapproving of them is a very threatening idea. It is as if their survival depends upon them "being good."

But this "being good" has a dark side. It is a compulsion, a drive from deep within the unconscious mind to compensate for an intrinsic lack of self-worth. Such a drive for approval can cause a co-dependent to give too much. A co-dependent person may give away all of their money, their time, their energy to another person, leaving themselves bereft and bankrupt financially, physically and/or emotionally. This is not love. This is compulsion.

Meister Eckhart, the great Christian mystic, delineated a difference between compulsion and compassion, which I think is a crucial key to discovering the difference between the pseudo-love of the co-dependent and the mystical love of one residing in level three awareness.

From his writings, we learn that Eckhart spent a lot of his time in level three and above. To him the world was filled with the wondrous all-consuming love of God, a love that was extended to all beings without distinction (a typical level three perception). From this exalted state of level three awareness, Meister Eckhart felt compassion for his fellow beings. He was filled with a deep love for them, but he was not driven by a compulsion to give himself away.

Indeed, as Matthew Fox points out in his book, titled *A Spirituality Named Compassion*, one can quite effectively use the continuum of compulsion vs. compassion to ascertain the spiritual maturity of a person or a society.

It is possible for someone who is co-dependent to transit into a level three awareness. In such a case the mystical altruism of this level would, most likely, mix in with his or her pseudo-love or compulsion.

However, in pure level three awareness there is no compulsion, only a deeply abiding compassion for self and others.

Such a state of pure compassion and interconnectedness with life can release strong emotions, especially in one who has previously been in a highly contracted state, such as level one. In fact, moving upwards from any of the levels can release emotions.

The feeling of losing boundaries as one moves upwards

along the spiral can be exhilarating or threatening, depending on the extent of one's control needs. It can also be threatening to those around the person who is transiting to a higher level on the spiral.

From the vantage point of level one or even level two awareness, my act of giving away "hard earned" money to a total stranger would seem to be the very essence of insanity.

I know of instances where well-intending family members have had someone hospitalized because he or she had moved to a higher level on the spiral than they were comfortable with. This situation is often complicated by the fact that a person transiting to a higher level often does not understand what is happening to him or her. And to complicate matters, our culture does not offer any plausible maps to explain what is happening. It is also during such experiences that the unconscious mind often "dumps" suppressed emotions and memories into conscious awareness. Such a wholesale dumping of "stuff" can make these situations ripe for a diagnosis for psychosis or some other mental condition.

Please note that I am not saying that anyone diagnosed as psychotic is merely transiting to higher levels of awareness. I am saying that in some cases, the diagnosis of a mental condition may be inaccurately given due to an inability of the person to integrate these experiences in a socially appropriate manner .

As one moves upwards along the spiral into level three and beyond, there seems to be an increase in the number of synchronicities for many people. I often hear such persons remarking that they find themselves in the right place at the right time, that miracles seem commonplace. As mental health professionals begin to study these transits into more expanded egoic states, we will come to better understand this phenomena. I suspect that it is a function of being open to a greater frame of intelligence that generates such synchronicities.

Life Upon the Great Sea Entering Level Four

It is at level four awareness that our ego has its most tenuous foothold. The immensity of life forces that confronts one can be awesome by level one standards. To the person equipped for such an experience it can be a beautiful and transformational event. However, for one whose psyche is ill prepared, the experience can be traumatic. I know this from personal experience.

Spring had come to the university campus, and I was sitting outside in the quad watching my fellow students playing tag football or stretched out on the ground catching some sun. For months, I had been practicing a secret Tibetan technique for the rapid expansion of consciousness with some interesting though unspectacular results. Although I was fatigued from studying for exams, and strung-out from three days without sleep, I decided to practice the meditation that afternoon.

I closed my eyes and began to focus my attention in the prescribed manner. Almost immediately, I heard and felt a buzzing sound next to my ear. I looked up and realized that the entire world had changed. Although everything looked the same, I could "see" through the walls of the high rise dorms. I could feel every feeling and experience every thought being experienced by the several hundred students within a five hundred foot radius. The experience was awesome. Tears came to my eyes. The sheer power of all those desires and experiences rushed through me. For an instant I did not know who I was. I had become lost in the great sea of life revealed before me.

It was then that I heard a kind of snap and my body temperature soared through the roof. I became deathly ill. Sweat poured from every pore. My clothes were suddenly soaking wet. I stood up. Some deep inner urge propelled me down the twisted path through the woods to the student infirmary. As I came out onto the sidewalk, I could barely walk. The buzzing sound whirled around my head.

On the way, my roommate and some of my friends passed me on their way to the cafeteria for lunch, and asked me if I wanted to join them. I couldn't answer. I had the distinct impression that they were in a movie. They were images on a two-dimensional screen, and I could not make contact with them. They walked past me.

Somehow I made it to the infirmary. When the attending nurse took my temperature she turned ashen white, told me to stay put, and in a few minutes the student doctor appeared and whisked me off to bed.

For three days and nights I existed in a feverish delirium. My bed had become a raft, and I was drifting through water. At times I would have the same recurring dream except I didn't know it was a dream.

I was driving some kind of old car through the desert as the sun was setting. Off in the distance, I could see a deserted adobe. I knew with every atom of my body that when I got there, someone would be waiting for me, and this someone would reveal to me the secrets of the universe. But as I got closer, the adobe retreated further off into the chaparral.

This went on for the three days of my delirium. Finally, when the fever subsided, I began to piece together what had happened.

Through the secret Tibetan technique, I had managed to slip past my usual buffers, aided no doubt by the extreme fatigue of having stayed up several nights in a row to cram for exams. I had, unwittingly, entered the fourth level of consciousness, and my body/psyche was simply not prepared for the intensity of such an occurrence. The weakest link in my psyche/body/mind had snapped and to my good fortune it was my body and not my mind that had given way.

My fever made it a medical condition. If I had not presented a fever, my delirious state of mind would have been interpreted as a psychotic break and instead of recuperating in the relative comfort of the infirmary (my room looked out over a grove of trees), I would have spent it in the mental wing of the university hospital.

In my understanding of the spiral, my first experiences in the quad were of pure fourth level. I was sensing life's energy and power directly. I could see and sense things that I could not sense in my normal states of awareness. Such abilities are called "siddhis," and many of the ancient yogic systems speak about these remarkable states with great clarity.

But it takes a tremendous amount of internal integrity or strength to sustain such experiences without damage. The buzzing in my ears was the sound of a primordial energy mapped out by earlier explorers of consciousness and is called Kundalini shakti. This serpent energy coiled up in the spine is usually latent. But due to my forceful opening it was stimulated into activity.

The fever that so concerned my doctors was, most likely, something called "psychic heat" given off by the premature rise of the serpent power within my own body.

The delirium I experienced was the result of my unconscious mind downloading its experiences, metaphors, and struggles into my conscious awareness. Had these contents of my perturbed mind been able to be integrated into my personal identity, they would have actually enriched my understanding of myself. But since mine was a "medical condition," no effort was given to address my mental experiences.

Let me balance out my description of level four lest the reader conclude that it is a very dangerous place. Actually, given the right situation, level four can be beatific.

Once, during an intense period of reading the sacred texts of several different religions, I became infused with a love for God. During the peak of this period, which lasted for about a week, I walked in a world of enchantment. Everywhere I looked, I saw and experienced only love. Everything shimmered with a kind of cosmic glow. My sense of self became more and more immersed in this love of God until I, as an individual, did not exist. I had become love itself. During this period it seemed that animals and children were inexplicably drawn to me, and I to them.

This period of intense, almost ecstatic bliss, ended on a rather funny note. I was walking towards a psychology class when all of a sudden I experienced two angels, one on either side walking with me towards the science building. At this point, I feared that I was becoming psychotic. The angels disappeared and did not return to my conscious awareness again for over twenty years.

The meeting of non-corporeal beings or entities is a common experience in expanded states of awareness, especially at level four and beyond. I will speak about these beings in a moment, but I want to come back to a crucial point about my premature experience with level four.

If you look at the Spiral of Consciousness, you will see that there is a line that goes up the middle with arrows that point back down towards level one.

The level of our consciousness is determined by many factors, and once achieved these levels are not static. They are constantly in flux. One reason for this state of flux is the law of polarities.

All systems attempt to find a state of equilibrium, including the body/mind. If we go too far out in either direction, we will find ourselves inexorably pulled back in the opposite direction. Thus someone who finds himself or herself propelled out into one of the higher levels of awareness may very well find himself or herself in a contracted state. My premature excursion into level four left me with a weakened physical and mental condition for several months.

One would do well to take heed from the adage: Storm not the gates of heaven, lest you find yourself in hell.

The Pantheon of the Upper Levels

It is a common experience at level four and beyond to experience non-corporeal beings or entities.

This is a touchy subject with many mental health professionals since one common thought is that such beings are pure hallucinations and are thus a signature of psychopathology.

The issue is made all the more difficult by the fact that sometimes a person is deluded (like Caressa) into thinking that an entity is real when it is, in fact, a projection of the unconscious mind. Still, all of this does not necessarily negate the existence of "real" non-corporeal beings.

All of the various spiritual disciplines and traditions speak on this. Many Christian saints reported seeing and communicating with angels. It is a sign of our overly materialistic and narcissistic age that these experiences are considered by most academics to be a form of delusion and are summarily dismissed.

The shamanic traditions from all cultures include an entire host of disincarnate beings, some of which are beneficial and others that are not.

It is not in the scope of this chapter to address the issues of ontological reality as they relate to these reported beings. However, it is a common experience of persons who enter higher levels of consciousness to run into such beings, whether they be pure projections or not.

Whether or not these beings are real does not diminish their power at higher levels of awareness. A god or goddess who appears to one in all of the deity's awesome power is something to be contended with. What may have seemed like a fascinating metaphor at levels one, two or three may emerge as a living and vibrating power at levels four and five. These beings can literally destroy one or give immeasurable blessings.

My personal view on the resident pantheon of the upper levels is one of pragmatism. During an experience with such beings, I operate as if they are absolutely real and to be accorded all the due respect such a position would entail.

When I return to one of the lower egoic states (one, two, or three), I analyze the experience to see what value it may have or what usable information it offers me in my day-to-day life. I include emotion in this category of information here, since I have found that encountering a benevolent being in one of these higher levels imparts a sense of well-being to me as I return to the lower levels of awareness.

Moving into Level Five

Level five occupies the largest volume of the spiral due to the immensity of space that one experiences at this level.

Each level of awareness has its own corresponding sense of space. At level one, we experience extreme egoic contraction and a resulting contracting of space. This lack of space may be experienced as a contracted sense of time or a sense of being "trapped" in the body. At level five, we move into an awesomely expansive space of cosmic proportions.

To explain the odd paradox that can occur at level five, I need to explain a polarity that occurs in consciousness. This polarity is that of observation vs. identification.

If we observe something, we are separate from it. If we identify with something, we become it to some extent. A parent who identifies with a child will feel that child's joy or that child's pain. A parent who merely observes the child will not share that child's experience.

This polarity exists on all levels of awareness. But as we move into level five its effects are most pronounced.

If we shift into a space of observation as we move into level five, we will have the experience of being a speck in a vast ocean of cosmic forces and beings. We will seem very small in comparison to the awesome powers that surround us. This can elicit in us a feeling of awe or terror depending on our tendencies.

If, however, we identify with the space around us as we shift into level five, we will completely lose our sense of a personal self. The space of level five is too vast for our nervous systems to hold, and we disappear as a reference point to ourselves in such a powerful state.

This state is called samadhi in yoga, and the early explorers of consciousness have mapped out several types of samadhi depending upon which of the upper levels one is transiting.

In samadhi, one loses one's outer awareness. The physical world, as we experience it day-to-day, disappears from our minds. We are immersed in a sea of primordial and cosmic energies. The individual consciousness of the person entering level five becomes like a drop of water entering a vast ocean.

While it may be difficult to talk in level four awareness, it is virtually impossible at level five or beyond. Consciousness so expands that the access to language or the motor areas of the brain become, at best, tenuous.

The most famous modern day person who entered level five and beyond was the Indian saint Ramakrishna. So immersed was he in level five experiences, he could often not eat or walk without assistance during his transits to these higher levels.

To the pragmatic, outwardly based Western mind this seems like a highly undesirable state. However, it is a world of incredible power.

For most of us, level five is unattainable. It requires a strength of psyche and a discipline that few are willing to develop. We must be content with those few explorers of consciousness who have brought and will continue to bring back reports of their strange and divine visions.

Dismantling the Universe: Moving Into Level Six

At level five one is in the most expanded state of awareness. Such an awareness may seemingly span the entire universe with all of its many beings and energies.

As we move into level six, we begin to experience the universe falling apart, falling into its fundamental energies. The great cosmic forces, the powerful gods and goddesses, the great Divinity itself is experienced as being made of fundamental energies.

There is no personal self at this level. There is only energy, *Purusha* the Hindus call it, the very stuff out of which the universe is made.

The Vedic Rishis of ancient India intuited this fundamental level of energy which they called the three gunas. The gunas are subtle energies, more subtle than any subatomic particle yet able to be detected by atomic physics. The gunas unfold, sustain, and destroy the universe.

At level six awareness, one has a direct experience of these forces. Gone are the personal gods and goddesses, gone is the self and all other beings, be they corporeal or non-corporeal. At this level of awareness, there is only energy, the dancing energy of the cosmos.

A crude analogy might serve us here in our understanding of level six. If you were to hold a rose in your hand at level one, two or three, you would say that you are holding a rose in your hand. At level four, you might say that the rose you were holding was pulsating with the same life force that was pulsating in you, that in some inexplicable way you and the rose were connected. You might even say that you loved the rose.

At level five awareness, you would probably be unable to hold the rose since your consciousness would have expanded beyond the person holding the rose. When you returned from level five, you might say that your experience of the rose was that it was part of a vast sea of energy and consciousness.

If you entered level six, however, your comment would be odd indeed. For you the rose, the universe, and all forms, including yourself, would have disappeared. There was no rose. There was no you, only the vibrating and oscillating fundamental energies of an undefined universe.

At level six, one is in the primordial pre-subatomic soup of the universe. One movement upward and the universe disappears!

The Cheshire Universe: Moving Into Level Seven

The Tibetan Buddhists call it the "fertile void."

It is a place from which everything manifest emerges, but is, itself, empty. This is a strange concept for Westerners who try to fill every empty space they can.

The void is a place of pure awareness without object. A person at level seven is aware that he is aware, but he does not have awareness of anything. The body is gone. The universe is gone. Everything is ultimately still. Time and space collapse. For one in this state, an hour can go by and will seem as if it has been a second.

Numerous studies have been done on meditators when they enter level seven awareness, and universally they stop breathing, their heart beats stop or slow down significantly, and muscle tension decreases along with blood pressure.

For meditators who access level seven, the world pops in and out of awareness. Only the most advanced human consciousnesses can stay in level seven for a long time. Most people who access this state do so fleetingly, maybe for a few seconds to a few minutes at a time. During that time, the world and their own sense of themselves disappears. They experience themselves as pure awareness floating in a sea of timeless stillness.

They are in the fertile void and in the most powerful level of awareness, the very substratum of the universe and consciousness itself. Then, when they least expect it, the world, like the Cheshire cat in *Alice in Wonderland* fades back into view.

Being in level seven awareness has many benefits. It is a profound state of rest, and studies have shown that such states of rest have very positive effects on health. There are many methods for entering level seven awareness. One of the most popular forms is TM or Transcendental Meditation, mentioned in Chapter 8. Another very effective method is the Taoist meditation "Heaven's Gate," also discussed in Chapter 8. The Buddhist "mindfulness" meditations can also lead one into Level Seven awareness.

Level seven awareness is odd in that most anyone can access it given the right method. I encourage the reader to pursue these methods since the benefits of level seven awareness are extensive.

I have personally found level seven awareness to be a very beneficial state. It definitely decreases the impact of stress, and I feel that it adds to my creativity and generally increases my mental performance.

Transits

Looking at the Spiral, you will see that there are dotted lines going from level to level. These transits denote that it is possible to "pop" from any of the levels to another level almost instantaneously.

This sometimes happens quite dramatically. A person suffering from a long or terminal illness may suddenly find themselves in a higher level. A psychological shock, accidents, drugs, some psychospiritual techniques and/or exhaustion may trigger a transit.

Remember that transits can go either way, from a contracted egoic state to an expanded cosmic state or back the other way.

Such transits can be exhilarating or fearful depending on what level one has entered and what his or her beliefs are about these types of experiences.

Handling Transit Emergencies

As I said at the beginning of this chapter, I believe that more and more people will be spontaneously experiencing higher levels of awareness and that some methodology is needed for helping these people. Such a methodology must, I feel, honor the person having these experiences without labeling them as sick or deranged.

The goal should be to allow the person to integrate his or her transpersonal experiences in a way that enriches his or her life.

If you are experiencing disruptions in your functioning due to one of these kinds of experiences or someone you know is, I advise you to find an "enlightened mental health professional." By "enlightened" I mean someone who isn't going to automatically assume that your experiences are pathological just because they are non-ordinary.

I have found acupuncture to be helpful for those going through an acute reactive stage (entering level one after being in level four or higher). This stage is often characterized by level one symptoms: anxiety, paranoia and isolation. The meridian system seems to be especially vulnerable to transits, and a good acupuncturist can help bring the body/mind back into balance.

I also strongly suggest some kind of psychotherapy to help integrate the massive amounts of material that usually arise from such an experience.

Final Words

By necessity, my discussion of this model (the Spiral of Consciousness) has been limited in this chapter. There are many subtle nuances and factors I have not discussed. For those interested in pursuing a greater understanding of these concepts, including other maps as laid out by other explorers of consciousness, I offer a small bibliography in Appendix C.

CHAPTER EIGHTEEN

The Future

"The future exists first in imagination, then in will, then in reality."
– Barbara Marx Hubbard

For those interested, the following discussion is primarily speculative in nature.

It is my belief that we are poised for a radical shift in our understanding of the brain's role in consciousness. I believe this shift will be no less dramatic in its impact than Copernicus' realization that the earth was not the center of the solar system.

The research in Near Death Experiences (NDEs), which I mentioned earlier, indicate that some part of our consciousness is independent of brain processing. How else could a person, pronounced clinically dead, come back from such an experience and recount the conversations of the doctors, nurses, and attendants?

And consider, if you will, the startling research of Valerie Hunt, Ph.D. In her rigorous studies of the human nervous system, she has measured the brain's EEG patternings to reach as high as 150 cps. However, she has measured another, more ephemeral, aspect of the human nervous system that reaches up to 200,000 cps.

She has called this energetic aspect of the human nervous system the "human energy field." It corresponds to, what is called by some esoteric schools, the aura.

Dr. Hunt has measured and quantified this energy field and found that it is more responsive to stimulation than the brain itself. In one study, she showed that the field was faster than the brain at picking up changes in the environment. If, for instance, someone were to enter the area where you are now reading, Dr. Hunt's research indicates that your energy field would sense the intruder's presence before your brain would, and that this field extends several feet outside your body.

Dr. Hunt's work, as well as that of many others, is uncovering a much more subtle mechanism of perception than we previously thought existed.

Research in the area of remote viewing is quite remarkable in that sensory perception seems to operate outside the known constraints of the central and peripheral nervous systems. In remote viewing, a person enters an altered state of consciousness and is then asked to "view" something at a given location far from the actual physical location of the subject.

In an uncanny number of instances, remote viewers have given accurate accounts of objects hundreds, sometimes thousands of miles from their own person.

The ability of consciousness to operate outside of time and space constraints is not limited to remote viewing. It is often seen in transpersonal events as well.

I recall a workshop several years ago where a woman suddenly and deeply forgave her mother who she had been estranged from for many years. During the next break, this woman called her mother. They had not spoken for years. Her mother reported that the thought of her daughter had suddenly and unexpectedly come to her about the time of her daughter's experience in the workshop. Not only this, but the mother spontaneously forgave her without knowing why. These two women lived two thousand miles a part.

I have seen similar events occur often in both group and individual settings. It seems that a predominant factor is the presence of powerful and coherent emotion such as unconditional love. When such emotion is present, time and space may become "fluid" and persons disconnected by hundreds or thousands of miles can suddenly feel as if they are intimately connected.

As research into subtle energy proceeds over the next decade, I suspect that we will find our views of consciousness vastly expanding. I think that we will discover that the brain is one part of a much larger "nervous system" and that this subtle nervous system is non-localized, multi-dimensional, and multi-gifted. Our consciousness may be much more extensive and un-bound than the brain through which it expresses itself.

There are "doors" in the brain through which we can enter these larger realms of consciousness, the un-bound if you will. These doors, are quite literally, the biochemical and electrical events of altered states.

With the tools you have mastered in this book, you can enter these realms for yourself and bring back treasures from your inner worlds. These treasures can enrich both your life and those around you through the creativity, insight and power they can bestow.

To those of you who choose to explore the uncharted seas of your own consciousness, know that you have embarked upon one of humanity's greatest adventures.

May we acknowledge and give solace to each other as we pass on the waters. And may we share our discoveries freely. For it is through the free exchange of information and insight that we will better be able to explore the Great Space of our own collective being.

The map makers, the ones who drafted the sailing routes for Columbus, Magellan, and the others, kept their maps secret. This is not a time for secrecy. It is a time to share knowledge. If mankind is to survive we must, as a species, reach into the uncharted waters of our selves. We must discover and bring out the greatest, the most noble and the most wondrous parts of our being. For in the end, that is the greatest gift we can give ourselves and the greatest legacy we can leave for those who follow.

APPENDIX A

Measuring Waves

If you were to go to the ocean and stand out at the end of a long fishing pier, you would be able to see the ocean waves from the side as they rolled onto shore.

Although each wave would be different, all waves would share common characteristics.

In the diagram below, you can see a typical sine wave pattern. The top of the wave is called the "peak," while the bottom of the wave is called the "trough." Waves are measured from peak to peak, and this is called one cycle.

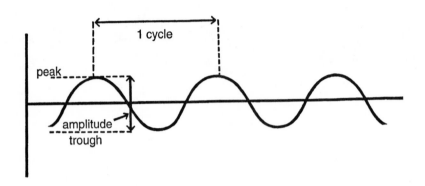

Figure 14

If you had a stopwatch with you, you could measure how fast the waves were rolling in to shore. For instance, you might find that six waves rolled past you in a minute on a calm day. We could express this measurement as 6 cpm or six cycles per minute. During a storm you might count as many as sixty waves passing in front of you in a minute. We could express this as 60 cpm.

Even though we can't see it, sound travels as a wave form. These sound waves travel so fast we must express them, not in cycles per minute (cpm), but in cycles per second (cps).

Cycles per second is a universal measurement that allows us to describe a wide range of pulsations including sound, light and electromagnetism (as in brain waves).

When used to measure sound, the term cps is often replaced by the term Hertz (Hz). These terms are interchangeable. In other words, 1 cps = 1 Hz.

In terms of pitch, the lower the number of Hz the lower the pitch. The higher the number of Hz, the higher the pitch.

Brain wave activity is also measured in terms of cps or Hz. The slower the wave activity within the brain, the more relaxed and less alert we feel. On the contrary, the faster the wave activity within the brain, the less relaxed and more alert we feel.

The brain has a very high water content and thus greatly facilitates electromagnetic wave activity. As in the ocean, waves continually rise and fall within the brain. These waves are created from cascades of electrical and magnetic activity, and our state of consciousness is mirrored in how these waves flow throughout the brain.

APPENDIX B

To obtain a free brochure listing the tapes developed by the author in the areas of stress, healing, accelerated learning, increased intelligence, creative problem solving, meditation, and the exploration of consciousness, call or write: Acoustic Brain Research's exclusive publisher-

Quantum Link
8665 East Miami River Rd.
Cincinnati, OH
513/ 353-4315

Within the United States, toll free:
1-800-531-9283

A Special Invitation to Readers of This Book:

In several of the exercises, the author mentions the use of a special brain entrainment tape, "Creative Imagining." This tape will assist you in entering more relaxed brain states, thus making the exercises easier to do.

Quantum Link, the exclusive Distributor of Acoustic Brain Research tapes, is offering readers of *Brain States* a special discount. By placing your order and identifying yourself as a reader of this book, you will get a 20% discount. The tape, normally $19.95, is available for $15.96 and shipping is $4.00 in the U.S. and $5.50 in Canada and Mexico.

To order your copy, call or write Quantum at the number/ address on previous page. Visa/Master Card customers may place their orders by phone.

Exercises Available on Audio Tapes

The author has developed a set of audio tapes entitled **Brain Power: Unlocking the Unlimited Potential of Your Mind** that guides the listerner through many of the techniques and concepts presented in this book. For further information, call or write:

Awakenings
3792 Haits Lake Rd.
Roy, WA 98580
Tel: 206-458-5347
Fax: 206-458-2923
Toll Free in the United States: 1(800) 870-1850

Seminars, Trainings and Certification Programs

To receive a listing of certified B/MR consultants, seminars, trainings, and professional certifications offered by the author, write:

Acoustic Brain Research
c/o Quantun Link
8665 East Miami River Road
Cincinnati, OH 45247
513-353-4315

Information about human energy fields

Dr. Valerie Hunt, the noted researcher mentioned several times in this book, has just recently released a series of video and audio tapes documenting her work with the human energy field and recorded sounds from the chakras. As this goes to press, these tapes are available on a donation basis only. Proceeds will go to further fund the work of Dr. Hunt's laboratory. To order, contact:

Bioenergy Fields Foundation
Post Office Box 4234
Malibu, CA 90265
310/457-4694

APPENDIX C

Resources

T he following partial list of resources is intended for those
readers who wish to deepen their understanding. The addresses of the publishers are not listed for those books easily
obtained through bookstores. Books which are more difficult to
track down are followed by the publisher's address.

Chapter 3   Pegasus and the Horse

The Amazing Brain, Robert Ornstein and Richard Thompson.
Houghton-Mifflin Company.

The Three Pound Universe: The Brain- From the Chemistry of the Mind to the New Frontier of the Soul, Judith Hooper and Dick Teresi. Dell.

The Triarchic Mind: A New Theory of Human Intelligence, Robert Sternberg. Viking.

Chapter 6   Tinker Toys of the Mind

Using Your Brain For A Change, Richard Bandler, Real People Press, pub.

Metamorphous Press, PO Box 10616, Portland, OR 97210
This publisher offers a complete listing of Neurolinguistic Programming related materials including excellent self-teaching programs.

Chapter 8 & 9 Stress Management/Inner Healer

Alphabet of the Heart, Dan Winter. Crystal Hill Farm, 9411 Sandrock Rd., Eden, NY 14057

(Note: An important book outlining significant discoveries concerning the role of emotion in health.)

Those exploring Dan Winter's fascinating work in psychophysiology may come across his material concerning the Hebrew and Arabic alphabets. Readers interested in this aspect of his work are urged to contact the Meru Foundation for information concerning Stan Tenin's work in this area as well. These two sources will give you the most complete picture of current advances in this intriguing subject. To contact Stan Tenin, write: The Meru Foundation, PO Box 1738, San Anselmo, CA, 94979.

Awaken Healing Light of the Tao, Mantak and Maneewan Chia.

Healing Tao Books. P.O. Box 1194, Huntington, NY 11743. This book is an excellent beginning resource for those interested in studying the use of Taoist yoga to improve health.

The Center for Professional Well-being, 21 West Colony Place, Suite 150, Durham, NC 27705-5596, 919/489-9167

Founded in 1979 by John-Henry Pfifferling, Ph.D., the Center focuses on mental health issues for professionals. Conducts trainings and conferences in stress management for professionals as well as one-on-one consulting around life transitions and career goals. An excellent resource.

Beyond OK: Psychegenic Tools to Health of Body and Mind, Win Wenger, Ph.D. Psychegenics Press, P.O. Box 332, Gaithersburg, MD 20760

The Healing Brain, Robert Ornstein, Ph.D. and David Sobel, M.D. Simon and Schuster.

Healing and The Mind, Bill Moyers. Doubleday.

Mind Your Health. 7605 1/2 West North Avenue, River Forest, This educational group conducts trainings and seminars based on cardiologist Dr. Bruno Cortis's work in preventive cardiology and medicine.

The Psychobiology of Mind - Body Healing, Ernst Rossi, M.D. Norton.

Super Immunity: Master Your Emotions and Improve Your Health, Paul Pearsall, Ph.D. Fawcett Gold Medal.

Taoist Yoga: Alchemy and Immortality, Lu Kuan Yu, Samuel Weiser, pub., Box 162, York Beach, Maine 03910.

This excellent source text on Taoist yoga is a translation of a major work by Taoist mater Chao Pi Ch'en who was born in 1860. It is from this text that the heaven's Gate Meditation was taken. A major find for those interested in this most fascinating of subjects.

Vibrational Medicine, Richard Gerber, M.D. Bear & Co.

Chapter 10   Increasing Intelligence

Beyond Teaching and Learning, Win Wenger, Ph.D. , Psychegenics Press, PO Box 332, Gaithersburg, MD, 20877.

This book is Dr. Wenger's most current treatise on accelerated learning and increased intelligence for the twenty-first century. A remarkable book with extensive methods and techniques that can be used by the reader for immediate benefit.

Project Renaissance: for information on seminars and materials created by Dr. Wenger, write Project Renaissance, P.O. Box 332, Gaithersburg, MD 20877.

The Creative Brain, Ned Hermann. Brain Books, c/o Applied Creative Services, 2075 Buffalo Creek Road, Lake Lure, NC, 28746.

Educational Kinesiology Foundation. PO Box 3396, Ventura, CA 93006-3396. Tel: Within the U.S. (1-800-356-2109). From Canada (805-658-7942).

This is the international center for EduK classes, seminars, books, and trainings. Call or write for a current schedule.

How To Increase Your Intelligence, Win Wenger, Ph.D. D.O.K. Publishers, PO Box 605, East Aurora, NY 14052

Use Both Sides of Your Brain, Tony Buzan. E.P. Dutton.

Whole Brain Thinking: Working From Both Sides of the Brain to Achieve Peak Job Performance, Jacquelyn Wonder and Priscilla Donovan. William Morrow.

Chapter 13   The Acoustic Brain

Cymatics, Hans Jenny, Basilius Presse. Available in the United States from MacroMedia, P.O. Box 279, Epping, NH 03042

The Conscious Ear, Alfred Tomatis. Station Press, pub.

The Cosmic Octave, Cousto. Life Rhythm Press, pub.

The Forgotten Power of Rhythm, Reinhard & Flatischler. Life Rhythm Press.

The Healing Forces of Music: History, Theory and Practice, Randall McClellan, Ph.D. Amity House.

Healing Sounds: The Power of Harmonics, Jonathan Goldman. *Mind, Music and Imagery*, Stephannie Merritt. Plume.

Music, Mind and Brain, Manfred Clynes, ed. Plenum Press.

Music and Miracles, compiled by Don Cambell. Quest Books.

Nada Brahma: the World Is Sound- Music and the Landscape of Consciousness, Joachim-Ernst Berendt. Destiny Books.

Rehabilitation, Music and Human Well-being, edited by Matthew M. Cee. M/MB.

Sound, Mind and Body: Music and Vibrational Healing, Macro-Media, P.O. Box 279, Epping, NH 03042.

This award winning video presents an excellent overview of the field of Sound Healing. MacroMedia is a very good source for hard to find videos and books on the subject. Write for a current listing.

Sounding the Inner Landscape: Music as Medicine, Kay Gardner. Caudecus Publications.

Chapter 14   Quantum Mind

The Holographic Universe, Michael Talbot. Harper Collins.

Info-Psychology, Timothy Leary. New Falcon Publications

Quantum Psychology, Robert Anton Wilson. New Falcon Publishing.

Stalking the Wild Pendulum, Itzhak Bentov. Bantam Books.

Star Wave: Mind, Consciousness and Quantum Physics, Fred Alan Wolf. Macmillan Publishing Company.

Chapter 15   Lucid Dreaming, Insomnia, and Things that Go Bump In the Night

Exploring the World of Lucid Dreaming, Stephen LaBerge, Ph.D. and Howard Rheingold. Ballantine Books.

Chapter 16   Brain Machines

MegaBrain, Michael Hutchinson, First Ballantine, pub.

Tools for Exploration
This resource center offers the most extensive listing of consciousness expansion machines, devices, tapes, and literature currently available. Call or write for their complete catalog.

Tools for Exploration
4460 Redwood Highway
Suite 2
San Rafael, CA 94903
1-800-456-9887

Chapter 17   Map for Explorers of Consciousness

Autobiography of A Yogi, Parmahansa Yogannanda. Self Realization Fellowship.
A look at the inner life and psychospiritual processes of a great yogi and teacher. Wonderful reading.

Development of the Psychedelic Individual: A Psychological Analysis of the Psychedelic State and Its Attendant Psychic Powers, John Curtis Gowan, professor emeritus, California State University Northridge. Published privately by the author: 1426 Southwind Circle, Westlake Village, CA 91361. This book is a well-documented compendium of a class of non-ordinary abilities known as siddhis or yogic powers. It is the best book on the subject that I have seen.

The Future of the Body: Explorations Into the Further Evolution of Human Nature, Michael Murphy. Tarcher, pub.
A comprehensive overview of non-ordinary human possibilities. The book is excellent and draws from numerous sources.

Operations of Increasing Order: And Other Essays on Exotic Factors of Intellect, Unusual Powers and Abilities, John Curtis Gowan. (See *Development of Psychedelic Individual* for address of author). Another excellent book, well-documented and full of insight into non-ordinary human abilities.

The Supreme Self, Swami Abhayanananda. Atma Books.
3430 Pacific Ave. SE, Suite A-6144, Olympia, WA 98501.
A fascinating personal account of an American yogi and his pursuit of non-ordinary awareness.

Index

More Books by
United States Publishing

ORDER FORM

NAME _____

ADDRESS _____

CITY _____

STATE/ZIP_____

PHONE_____

❏ **Meditations for Transformation**   **$11.95**
Larry Moen
ISBN 1-880698-33-1

❏ **Meditations for Healing**   **$11.95**
Larry Moen
ISBN 1-880698-69-2

❏ **Meditations for Awakening**   **$11.95**
Larry Moen
ISBN 1-880698-77-3

❏ **Dear God**   **$12.00**
Larry Moen
ISBN 1-880698-09-9

Shipping   **$3.00**

TOTAL _____

Make checks payable and return with order form to:

United States Publishing
3485 Mercantile Avenue • Naples, Florida 33942
(813) 643-7787